How did it all begin—
    Human life and love?
    Marriage and family?
    Work and play?
    Food and drink?
    Pleasure and delight?
    Sin and its consequences . . .?
        Fractured human relationships?
        Alienation from God?
        Divine judgment?
        Death?

How It All Began introduces answers from Genesis 1-11, concerning the most vital issues and questions we face in life.

How It All Began

A Bible Commentary for Laymen/Genesis 1—11
BY RONALD YOUNGBLOOD

GL Regal Books A Division of G/L Publications
Ventura, California, U.S.A.

Other good Regal reading in
the Bible Commentary for Laymen Series:
Faith of Our Fathers (Genesis 12—50)
   by Ronald Youngblood
Highlights of the Bible (Genesis—Nehemiah)
   by Ray C. Stedman
Themes from the Minor Prophets
   by David Hubbard

The foreign language publishing of all Regal books is under the direction
of GLINT. GLINT provides financial and technical help for the adapta-
tion, translation and publishing of books in more than 85 languages for
millions of people worldwide.

For more information write: GLINT, P.O. Box 6688, Ventura, California 93006.

Published by Regal Books
A Division of G/L Publications
Ventura, California 93006
Printed in U.S.A.

Library of Congress Catalog Card No. 80-50539
ISBN 0-8307-0675-5

Contents

A Teacher's Manual and Student Discovery Guide for Bible study groups using *How it All Began* are available from your church supplier.

PREFACE

How old is the world? Who made the stars? Where did I come from? Questions like these are asked not only by little children but also, at various levels of understanding, by every thinking person. The book you are now about to read does not claim, by any means, to answer such questions fully. We do propose, however, to give responses that we trust will prove helpful in leading the way toward more complete answers. In other words, our book addresses the general topic of how it all began—the universe, the earth, life, sin, redemption, marriage, civilization, society, and much more.

Genesis 1—11 has no peer as a source book for providing answers to questions like these. Inspired by the Holy Spirit, the first several chapters of Scripture deal with the most vital issues that we face in life. And they do so in terms of real people confronting real problems in real historical situations. The following brief commentary on those remarkable chapters is merely one attempt to get at the questions they pose and the answers they give.

The notes at the end of most chapters and the bibliography at the end of the book are but a small sampling of the resources available to the reader who wishes to study Genesis 1—11 in a more extensive way. My personal debt of gratitude to all the students of Genesis who have preceded me can never be repaid. Their work has helped mine beyond measure, and I can only hope that mine will help future students in however small a way.

My special thanks go to the publishers of Regal books, who asked me to write this volume as a companion to my *Faith of Our Fathers* (a similar commentary for laymen on Genesis 12—50). Such confidence on their part is deeply appreciated.

Ronald Youngblood

1
INTRODUCTORY MATTERS

Genesis 1:1—11:26

How extraordinary the Bible is! It would be remarkable enough if it were merely a *human* book. But the fact that it is *God's* Word makes it all the more amazing. And to think that a loving God has condescended to speak to His often unlovely (and unlovable) creatures through Holy Scripture is enough to stagger the imagination.

Nevertheless, that is exactly what God has done. In the Bible the words may be human, but the voice is divine. The prophets and apostles who spoke and wrote the words of Scripture were "carried along by the Holy Spirit" (2 Pet. 1:21) like sailing vessels driven by the wind. Divine authority resides in what they said and wrote because their message is "not the word of men, but . . . the word of God" Himself (1 Thess. 2:13). As God's works of creation were made "by the breath of his mouth"

(Ps. 33:6), so also God's Word, from beginning to end, is "God-breathed" (2 Tim. 3:16).

It will be our privilege, in the course of this study, to see and hear what God is saying to us in the first few chapters of His Word. The opening sentences and paragraphs of any book are all-important for a proper understanding of what the book is saying because they set the stage for everything that follows. It is supremely important, then, that we pay careful attention to these early chapters of Genesis, the book that serves as such a magnificent introduction to the entire Bible.

Although we will start at the beginning, our journey will not take us quite through to the end of the eleventh chapter. More precisely, we will be studying Genesis 1:1—11:26. The reasons for stopping at Genesis 11:26 will become clear in a moment. For now, suffice it to say that the story told in these early chapters of Genesis has no equal elsewhere in world literature, and the events related in them have no parallel elsewhere in world history. This section of the Bible outlines for us the first steps in holy history and tells us how it all began.

Name: In the Beginning

Nearly the entire Old Testament was originally written in the Hebrew language, and Genesis is no exception. The Hebrew title of Genesis is *Bĕrēshîth* (pronounced bray-SHEATH), which means "in the beginning." In ancient times a book was almost always named after its first two or three words, a practice still followed in some cases (hymns and papal encyclicals, for example). With respect to Genesis it was especially appropriate because Genesis is indeed the book of beginnings.

The Hebrew Old Testament was eventually translated

into the Greek language (beginning about 250 years before the time of Christ) so that people whose native tongue was Greek could have the Word of God in their own language. The Greek translators then gave their own title, *Genesis*, to the first book of their Old Testament text. This word, identical to the English title which is derived from it, is a form of the word *geneseōs* (pronounced geh-NEH-seh-oas), found in the Greek translation at Genesis 2:4 and 5:1 (and, significantly, in Matthew 1:1). Depending on its context the word means birth, genealogy, history of the origin, and the like. Again, the Greek and English title is entirely appropriate, because Genesis is indeed a history book of origins, of births, of genealogies—of "how it all began."

Purpose: Why the Israelites Went to Egypt

The Old Testament as a whole tells the story of the Hebrew people—who they were, where they lived, what they did, how they acted. The book of Exodus describes in detail the great redemptive event in their history prior to the first coming of Jesus Christ: their miraculous release from slavery in Egypt, the greatest world power of that time. The book of Genesis, on the other hand, tells us why the Hebrew people—or, more specifically, the family of Jacob (also known as Israel)—went down to Egypt in the first place.

To put it in another way, Genesis was written from the standpoint of the Exodus. It is as if the newly-freed Israelite slaves asked their leader Moses, "How did we get here?" and then Moses told them the story of their forefathers, the patriarchs Abraham, Isaac, Jacob and Joseph, culminating with the account of how Joseph, one of Jacob's sons, was sold into slavery in Egypt by his brothers and how the rest of the family joined him there later. That story forms the so-called patriarchal history of Genesis 12—50 (or, more precisely, 11:27—50:26).

But that exciting tale would only whet the appetites of the Israelites even further. We can easily picture them as immediately asking another question: "Where did the patriarchs come from?" And another: "What happened before that?" And another—and so on, and so on, and so on! For our part, we can be grateful that God condescended to reveal to His servant Moses the answers to questions that he and his fellow Israelites were asking. We can be fairly sure that Moses shared their insatiable curiosity, because Genesis 1:1—11:26 is the glorious result. And as Genesis 11:27—50:26 is often called the *patriarchal history* because of its clearly defined subject matter, so also is Genesis 1:1—11:26 often called the *primeval history* because of its equally clear theme: It tells us about the beginning of the universe, of the heavenly bodies, of the earth with its seas and lakes and rivers and streams and mountains and hills, of inanimate plant life, of animate life including water creatures and air creatures and land creatures.

Most important of all, Genesis 1:1—11:26 tells us about the beginning of human life and love, of marriage and family, of work and play, of food and drink, of pleasure and delight. And unfortunately—on the darker side—we also learn about the beginning of sin and its consequences: fractured human relationships, alienation from God, divine judgment, and death.

All of this we will find as we make our way through the action-packed and lesson-filled pages of the primeval history found in the first 11 chapters of Genesis. And I would stress the word *our,* because Genesis 1:1—11:26

describes the origins not only of the Israelite people but of us as well. Their history is ours, and we were there along with them.

How amazingly comprehensive and all-inclusive is the "it" in the phrase "how it all began"!

Authorship: Moses

Until the seventeenth century after Christ, Jewish and Christian scholars alike were virtually unanimous in their opinion that Moses was the author (or at least the compiler) of the first five books of the Old Testament (including, of course, Genesis). That section was known as the five books of Moses and, in order to keep anything from being added to it or subtracted from it, Jewish tradition referred to it as the five-fifths of the law, that is, the Law of Moses.

But then in 1670 Benedict Spinoza, a Spanish Jew of scholarly repute, published his views regarding the authorship of those five books (known also as the *Pentateuch*, a word of Greek origin that means, simply, five-volumed book. Spinoza was of the opinion that the Pentateuch was compiled by Ezra (the author, or compiler, of the Old Testament books of Ezra and Nehemiah, and perhaps the compiler of 1 and 2 Chronicles as well). He felt that no competent author would write about himself in the third person (Moses is almost always depicted in the third person in the Pentateuch) or describe his own death (see Deut. 34:5-8).

Such arguments, however, are not difficult to counter. It was common literary practice in ancient times for authors to frequently refer to themselves in the third person in their writings, as Julius Caesar did in his *Gallic Wars*, for example. In fact, Ezra himself, in the book that bears his name, writes of himself sometimes in the third person (see Ezra 7:1-11) and sometimes in the first person (see 7:27—8:1). Also, it is said of Ezra that he was "a teacher well versed in the Law of Moses" (7:6) and that he "had devoted himself to the study and observance of the Law of the LORD, and to teaching its decrees and laws in Israel" (7:10). In short, the Bible describes Ezra as a student and teacher of the Law of Moses (that is, the Pentateuch), not its author or compiler.

As for the argument that no writer could compose his own obituary after the fact, that is readily granted. But just because Moses did not write Deuteronomy 34 does not mean that he did not write the rest of the Pentateuch. Old Testament books may have a concluding paragraph or chapter that was written by someone other than the main author. Jeremiah is a clear example of this practice. Jeremiah 51:64 concludes as follows: "The words of Jeremiah end here"—and then comes chapter 52 of the book. A secretary or other friend of the author often added his own divinely inspired ending to a biblical book. In Moses' case, it may very well have been Joshua who wrote Deuteronomy 34.

In any event, the arguments of Spinoza and his followers are by no means sufficient to overthrow the long-held traditional view that Moses was the Pentateuch's author or compiler. Even though the negative opinions of Spinoza and others eventually unleashed a series of attacks against the Mosaic authorship of the Pentateuch on every conceivable basis (style, vocabulary, language, and so forth), which continue unabated down to our own time, conservative scholars have responded forcefully and adequately to all such objections. More to the point, they maintain that Mosaic authorship best accounts for all the evidence and that, in fact, Scripture itself teaches that

Moses was the author of all (or at least most) of the Pentateuch (see, among many passages that could be listed, Exod. 17:14; Deut. 31:24; Josh. 8:31; 2 Kings 14:6; Rom. 10:5; 2 Cor. 3:15; and—perhaps most impressive of all—the words of Jesus in John 5:45-47).

Although Moses' name is nowhere mentioned in Genesis itself, it follows that if he wrote the Pentateuch he also wrote Genesis. Furthermore Acts 15:1, which describes circumcision as a "custom taught by Moses," probably intends to refer to the detailed account in Genesis 17 where the rite of circumcision is initiated for the Hebrew patriarchs and their descendants, since nowhere else in the Pentateuch are the regulations for circumcision given.

And so, when all is said and done, I concur with the traditional view of the authorship of the first book of the Bible implied in the heading of that book as found, for example, in the *Revised Standard Version:* "The First Book of Moses, Commonly Called Genesis."

Date: Fifteenth Century B.C.

If Moses indeed wrote Genesis, then it goes without saying that the book was written during his lifetime. By everyone's calculations Moses lived at some time in what archaeologists call the Late Bronze Age (about 1550 to 1200 B.C.).

The precise dates of Moses' life are tied in with one of the most vexing problems of Old Testament chronology: the date of the Exodus. Although many dates for that important event have been proposed, the two most widely held are 1445 B.C. and 1290 B.C. For quite some time the 1290 date has had formidable arachaeological data on its side, relating primarily to evidence for the Israelite conquest of various towns and cities in Canaan. But the dating and interpretation of that evidence has recently become increasingly ambiguous, and at the same time other archaeological evidence (primarily from Ebla in northern Syria) has tended to push back the dating of the patriarchal period. These factors in particular have strengthened the position of those who hold to the 1445 date—a date that, in any case, fits better with a literal understanding of the internal biblical chronology than the 1290 date does. According to 1 Kings 6:1, Solomon began to build the Temple in the fourth year of his reign over Israel, which was "the four hundred and eightieth year after the Israelites had come out of Egypt." The fourth year of Solomon's reign was about 966 B.C., and 480 years before that would give us a date of about 1445 for the Exodus.

Israel's wanderings in the Sinai desert, under the leadership of Moses, would then have taken place during the 40 years immediately following 1445 B.C. And so it would seem safe to assume that Moses—a man suitably qualified for the task in terms of possessing the necessary education, motivation, energy and time—wrote the Pentateuch, including the book of Genesis, late in the fifteenth century before Christ.

Literary Structure

No great piece of literature—whether sacred or secular, whether inspired by God or not—comes about by accident. Students in literature courses in high school and college learn very soon that poems, short stories, essays, novels, historical accounts, and all other types of formal writing for artistic purposes are carefully crafted and are designed to be esthetically attractive as well as intellectually informative. A good writer will always try to stimulate the eye as well as the mind. He wants to appeal to his readers' sense of order and symmetry while he is teaching or entertaining them.

This is why students of literature spend so much time analyzing classic examples of prose and poetry in attempts to discover rises and falls in plot, to reconstruct the outline that was in the mind of the original writer, and to understand the literary devices used by the writer to get his main point or points across. Whether it be Chaucer's *Canterbury Tales* or Shakespeare's *King Lear* or Poe's *The Pit and the Pendulum* or Melville's *Moby Dick* or Steinbeck's *The Grapes of Wrath* or Haley's *Roots,* an author's work will be better understood and a reader's experience will be more satisfying if the reader takes time to learn a little something about literary structure and, more specifically, about the literary structure of the poem or prose account he is reading at the moment. In other words, knowing something about the *form* of a piece of literature will always help the reader gain a deeper understanding of the *contents* of that piece.

And this principle holds true for the Bible as well. It is helpful to know that many of Paul's epistles contain a doctrinal section followed by a section that stresses Christian conduct flowing out of the doctrines taught; see, for example, Romans, 2 Corinthians, Galatians, Ephesians, Colossians. To observe that the dramatic poetic dialogues that constitute the heart of the book of Job are sandwiched in between a prose introduction and a prose conclusion will heighten the reader's feelings of suspense and excitement. To perceive that the book of Deuteronomy is structured along the lines of an ancient political treaty, with the sovereign (God, in this case) demanding certain obligations (based on mutual respect and loyalty) from His people, helps the reader comprehend more fully the legally binding basis of God's relationships to Israel.

So literary structure, and the order and arrangement implied, is a useful tool to have in hand as we follow any author's line of argument, in the Bible or elsewhere. It will be especially useful to us as we plan our course of study in Genesis 1—11.

As we stated earlier in this chapter, the Greek word *genesis* (a form of which appears in Gen. 2:4 and 5:1) gives the English translation of the book its title. But it also proves to be the key to the literary structure of Genesis.

The entire book is divided into two unequal halves: 1:1—11:26 and 11:27—50:26. Each half has five sections, and each section is introduced by the phrase "This is the account of . . . " or its equivalent. The second half of Genesis, the so-called *patriarchal history*, exhibits the phrase at 11:27; 25:12; 25:19; 36:1 (repeated for emphasis at 36:9), and 37:2.

The first half of the book, the so-called *primeval history*, displays that same characteristic phrase at 2:4; 5:1; 6:9; 10:1; and 11:10. In addition, the Creation narrative of 1:1—2:3 forms the introduction to the primeval history as well as to the book of Genesis as a whole.

Outline

Thus the very word *genesis*, translated as genealogy or history of the origin or account, is both the title of the book of Genesis and the key word in unlocking its literary outline, as the following structural sketch of Genesis 1:1—11:26 shows:

I. Introduction (1:1—2:3)
II. Body (2:4—11:26)
   A. The account of the heavens and the earth (2:4—4:26)
   B. The written account of Adam's line (5:1—6:8)
   C. The account of Noah (6:9—9:29)
   D. The account of Shem, Ham and Japheth (10:1—11:9)
   E. The account of Shem (11:10-26)

From this basic literary outline of the primeval history we derive the following thematic outline for our own teaching purposes (without, of course, violating the literary outline that comes right from Genesis itself):

I. Creation: I (1:1—2:3)
   A. Introduction (1:1,2)
   B. Body (1:3-31)
   C. Conclusion (2:1-3)
II. Creation: II (2:4-25)
III. The Fall (3:1-24)
IV. The Rapid "Progress" of Sin (4:1-16)
V. Two Genealogies (4:17—5:32)
   A. The Genealogy of Pride (4:17-24)
   B. The Genealogy of Death (4:25—5:32)
VI. The Extent of Sin Before the Flood (6:1-8)
VII. The Great Flood (6:9—9:29)
   A. Preparing for the Flood (6:9—7:10)
   B. Judgment and Redemption (7:11—8:19)
      1. The prevailing of the waters (7:11-24)
      2. The abating of the waters (8:1-19)
   C. The Flood's Aftermath (8:20—9:29)

2
CREATION I

Genesis 1:1—2:3

The Genesis account of creation is set forth in two parts. The first (1:1—2:3) is written in measured and majestic prose and in a formal—almost liturgical—style. Its broad panorama is cosmic in its sweep and includes the visible universe as seen by the naked eye. The second (2:4-25), on the other hand, zeroes in on a small area of the earth's surface (the Garden of Eden) and depicts God's relationship with one human couple (Adam and Eve).

Introduction (Gen. 1:1,2)

On the western exterior wall of Breyer Hall, the chemistry and geology building at Wheaton College, these words are inscribed:

IN THE BEGINNING
GOD
CREATED THE HEAVENS
AND THE EARTH

On February 5, 1971, Apollo 14 commander Edgar Mitchell deposited on the moon a microfilm packet containing (1) a complete Bible and (2) one verse of the Bible written out in 16 languages. The words of that verse: "In the beginning God created the heavens and the earth."

A distinguished scientist-philosopher of a previous generation, after a lifetime of study and synthesis, asserted that the four fundamental determinations of physics are "time, space, substance, and causality."[1] Permit me to observe that those four basic concepts, and no more, are found in one verse of the Bible: "In the beginning [time] God created [causality] the heavens [space] and the earth [substance]."

One could scarcely think of a more suitable way to begin the Bible than with those majestic words, which teach us that God is the Creator of all that exists and that He brought the universe into being at a time so long ago that it staggers the imagination. No one knows for certain, of course, when the beginning was. But the Old Testament is far more interested in the *fact* of creation than in the *time* of creation, and the simple truth that God's creative activity took place during an indeterminate time known as "the beginning" was joyfully celebrated by poet (Ps. 102:25) and prophet (Isa. 40:21) alike.

The Gospel of John starts with the same words: "In the beginning." The first 10 verses of that Gospel stress the activity of Jesus Christ in creation. Not only our Redeemer, the Lord Jesus is also our Creator. As John puts it, "In the beginning . . . the Word [Jesus] was with God, and the Word was God" (John 1:1).

But how is that possible? How can a person be *with* someone and at the same time *be* that someone? Although our finite minds cannot understand such matters completely, the first verse of Genesis itself provides us with a helpful clue. It tells us that "God created." The noun *God* is plural but the verb *created* is singular. The Bible clearly teaches that God is one being, a unity (see Deut. 6:4; 1 Cor. 8:4). At the same time, the Bible just as clearly teaches that the one God exists in three Persons and is therefore also a trinity (see Matt. 28:19; 2 Cor. 13:14). And it would seem that all three Persons were active in Creation from the beginning: the Father (Gen. 1:1; John 1:1,2), the Son (the "Word," John 1:3,10), and the Holy Spirit (Gen. 1:2).

God made everything, with one exception: Himself. Although everything else had a beginning, He has always been (Ps. 90:2). In the Bible His existence is never debated; it is always assumed. And no conditions whatever are placed on His existence. "The God who made the world and everything in it . . . is not served by human hands, as if he needed anything, because he himself gives all men life and breath and everything else" (Acts 17:24,25). We are completely dependent on Him for every breath we take, but He is absolutely independent of the universe He has created.

Create is a very special verb in the Old Testament. It always has God as its subject; it is never used of human activity. We may make or form or fashion, but only God creates. In Genesis 1 the verb create is used sparingly. We are told that God created "the heavens and the earth" (the universe; 1:1), "the great creatures of the sea" (animate life; 1:21), and "man" (human life; 1:27). So that special verb is reserved for the most crucial items in God's program of creation. It is not used indiscriminately.

Old Testament Hebrew had no word for *universe,* so it used "the heavens and the earth" instead. That phrase is one of the biblical ways of saying "all things" (Eccles. 11:5; Isa. 44:24; Jer. 10:16; John 1:3) since everything that exists is either on earth or in the heavens (broadly conceived).

Before we leave Genesis 1:1, we should remind ourselves that it is not merely a stiff and formal statement about creation. Its teaching is intended to encourage us about who we are and where we come from, and its emphasis is oriented toward life rather than death, as Isaiah 45:18 comments so beautifully: "God . . . did not create [the earth] to be empty, but formed it to be inhabited." So it is somewhat ironic that the book of Genesis itself, which starts with that majestic phrase, "In the beginning God," ends with a phrase that reeks with the smell of death: "in a coffin in Egypt."

Genesis 1:2 concentrates on the earth and stresses the world-centered approach of the author. The earth rather than the heavens is the object of his interest at this point. After all, the earth is, in the words of J.B. Phillips, the "visited planet." For reasons that are hidden in His own sovereign wisdom, the God who created this incredibly vast universe chose to lavish special attention and care on a tiny planet in a small solar system located in the galaxy known as the Milky Way, itself an island universe shaped like a lens and estimated to be 100,000 light years across. When it is realized that millions of such galaxies exist in the universe proper, we cannot even begin to comprehend the rationale behind God's choice of us to be His "chosen people," belonging to Him alone (1 Pet. 2:9).

Darkness filled ancient man with nameless horror (see Amos 5:18,20), and the deep terrified him as well (see Jon. 2:3,5)—perhaps partially because the Babylonians deified it and worshiped it as a mythological dragon of the watery chaos. But neither darkness nor the deep is to be feared, since both were created by a loving God. The oceans are part of the earth that He made, and He Himself says, "I form the light and create darkness" (Isa. 45:7). At the time of creation "the Spirit of God" was there to give life to the lifeless, "hovering over the waters" like a bird that provides for and protects its young (see Deut. 32:10,11; Isa. 31:5). The creative power of that same Holy Spirit continues to be exerted today (see Job 33:4; Ps. 104:30).

"Formless and empty" in Genesis 1:2 is an English translation of Hebrew *tōhū wā-bōhū* pronounced TOE-hoo wah-BOE-hoo), a rhythmic and eye-catching phrase that pictures the situation on earth before it was touched by the creative hand of God (it occurs elsewhere only in Jer. 4:23). As it turns out, the phrase itself is the key that unlocks the literary structure of the rest of Genesis 1: The acts of separating and gathering on days 1-3 give form to the formless, and the acts of making and filling on days 4-6 give divine assurance that the heavens and the earth will never again be "empty."

Body (Gen. 1:3-31)

"And/Then God said" appears a total of nine times in the first chapter of Genesis (1:3,6,9,11,14,20,24,26,29) and, when used in conjunction with the phrase "formless and empty" mentioned above, gives us the following outline for Genesis 1:

Days of Forming	*Days of Filling*
1. "light" (1:3)	4. "lights" (1:14)
2. "water under the expanse" (1:7)	5. "every living and moving thing with which the water teems" (1:21)
3a. "dry ground" (1:9)	6a'. "livestock, creatures

that move along the ground, and wild animals" (1:24)

6a″. "man" (1:26)

3b. "vegetation" (1:11)

6b. "every green plant for food" (1:30)

The characteristic verbs that tie together days 1-3 are *separate* and *gather*—verbs of formation—while the verbs that unite days 4-6 are *teem* and *fill* and *be fruitful* and *increase* —verbs of filling.

But we would also observe that comparisons between the days can be made horizontally as well as vertically, as the outline indicates. *Light* is the key word on day 1, and *lights* is the key word on day 4. On day 2 God "separated the water under the expanse from the water above it," while on day 5 He said, "Let the water [under the expanse] teem with living creatures, and let birds fly above the earth across the expanse of the sky" (v. 20). In other words, on day 2 God separated the lower waters from the upper waters and on day 5 He created animals to inhabit the lower waters and then others to inhabit the upper waters.

Days 3 and 6 are different from the other days in Genesis 1 since both of them are climactic. Each uses the phrase "And/Then God said" more than once (day 3 twice, day 6 three times). Two additional comparisons can be made between days 3 and 6. On day 3 *dry ground* appeared, and on day 6 God made (1) "livestock, crea-tures that move along the ground, and wild animals," and (2) "man" to inhabit the dry ground. In addition, day 3 witnessed the covering of the earth with a carpet of "vegetation," while on day 6 God said that He would give to both man and animals "every green plant for food."

These striking horizontal and vertical relationships between the various days can hardly be accidental. On the contrary, they demonstrate the literary beauty of the chapter and emphasize the symmetry and orderliness of God's creative activity. But the obviously careful planning and thought that went into the crafting of such a tightly woven account cause us to raise a question that may help solve a problem or two in the chapter: Is it possible that the order of events in the Genesis 1 story of creation is partly literary and only partly chronological?

Without being at all dogmatic about it, we would like to suggest that this may be the case. If those English versions that translate the final words in Genesis 1:5,8,13,19,23 and 31 as "the first day," "the second day," "the third day," "the fourth day," "the fifth day" and "the sixth day" respectively are correct, then of course the case is closed. Such language demands that the author intends chronological order. But the fact is that the literal rendering of the Hebrew phrases in question would be as follows: "one day," "a second day," "a third day," "a fourth day," "a fifth day" and "the sixth day." We would point out that the omission of the definite article *the* from all but the sixth day allows for the possiblity of random or literary order as well as rigidly chronological order.

We would stress the fact that *nonchronological* does not mean *nonhistorical*. The book of Jeremiah, for example, is arranged in topical rather than chronological order, even though it is historical from beginning to end. Similarly, the two historical accounts of the temptation of Jesus by Satan in Matthew 4:1-11 and Luke 4:1-13 arrange the three crucial phases of the temptation in differing orders, indicating that either Matthew's order or Luke's is nonchronological.

Genesis 1—11 itself contains a clear example of non-chronological order. Genesis 10 depicts various peoples "spread out into their territories by their clans within their nations, each with its own language" (10:5), and then Genesis 11:1-9 tells the antecedent story of how that situation came about.

If the Genesis 1 creation account is at least partly nonchronological, several puzzling problems can be easily solved. For example, how can it be that God "separated the light from the darkness" and that He "called the light 'day' and the darkness . . . 'night' " on day 1 (1:4,5) if the sun was not created until day 4? The simplest answer would seem to be that these two days are not related to each other chronologically but that they both refer to the same event—the creation of the sun. Indeed, this would seem to be implied in 1:17,18 where it is stated that God set the sun "in the expanse of the sky . . . to separate light from darkness" (the latter phrase, in fact, is quoted directly from 1:4).

Or, to take another example, how can there be evening and morning (see 1:5,8,13) before the sun is brought into existence? If chronological order is not demanded, that is no longer a problem. Or again: How can plants—including fruit trees—which require photosynthesis for their very existence survive apart from sunlight (see 1:12,13)? The answer is best sought along these lines: The creation of the sun preceded the creation of plant life, providing warmth for the soil together with all the other conditions that would foster growth.

We would not, of course, *insist* that the days of Creation in Genesis 1 be understood as displaying non-chronological arrangement. We merely suggest it as a possible theory to help explain the difficulties that arise when the reader insists that the order must be chronological.[2]

Let us now turn to a discussion of the details of the individual days in sequence.

Day 1: God had only to speak and all things came into being (see Ps. 33:6,9; Heb. 11:3). He simply "commanded and they were created" (Ps. 148:5). Among the things He said is one of the choicest statements in Scripture: "Let there be light." These are the first recorded words of God in the Bible and they are cited in 2 Corinthians 4:6 as an illustration of the spiritual light that illumines the hearts of believers in Christ. Light often symbolizes the nature and glory of God in the Bible (see 1 John 1:5; Rev. 21:23).

Everything that God creates is "good" (see Gen. 1:4,9,12,18,21,25)—although there is a strange silence on this point in the account of the creation of man on day 6. Although fully aware of man's original state of perfection (as the story of the fall of man in chapter 3 demonstrates), perhaps the author could not bring himself to declare man good in the light of his own highly developed understanding of man's propensity for doing evil. Be that as it may, Genesis 1:31 stamps the whole of God's creation as "very good," and that summary statement obviously includes man. And just as all that God has made is good, so is He good to all He has made (see Ps. 145:9).

When God gave names to the light and the darkness by calling them "day" and "night" (see also 1:8,10), He was declaring His sovereignty and rulership over them. To name something or someone in ancient times implied dominion or ownership (2 Kings 23:34; 24:17). Day and night alike belong to the Lord (Ps. 74:16).

Day 2: The "expanse" is the visible atmosphere or sky (see Gen. 1:8), characterized by the layer of clouds that contain the water above it (1:7; Ps. 148:4). The older translation, "firmament," gives a false impression of the nature of the expanse. Phrases such as "hard as a mirror" (Job 37:18) and "like a canopy" (Isa. 40:22) are merely highly picturesque ways of describing it.

"And it was so" is the only possible outcome, whether stated (see Gen. 1:7,9,11,15,24,30) or implied, to God's "Let there be." He speaks and it is done, whether in heaven or on earth.

"One place" (1:9) is a vivid way of describing the location of the "seas" (1:10) that surround the dry ground on all sides and into which the lakes and rivers flow. The earth was "founded . . . upon the seas" (Ps. 24:2) and "formed out of water" (2 Pet. 3:5). The waters of the seas are not to cross the boundaries God has set for them (see Ps. 104:7-9; Jer. 5:22).

Day 3: Genesis 1:11 teaches that creation, although ultimately a divine act, sometimes took place through secondary means (see also 1:24). At the same time, the Bible categorically rules out the possibility of evolution on the grand scale overwhelmingly claimed for it by its supporters. Plants and animals alike were to reproduce only within categories called "kinds" (1:11,12,21,24,25) that were carefully distinguished from each other.

Day 4: Although for unbelievers the lights in the sky may be sources of terror (Jer. 10:2), for God's people they serve as signs to mark off periods of time (Gen. 1:14; Psa. 104:19).

Why are the sun and moon called the "two great lights" in Genesis 1:16? Perhaps the words *sun* and *moon* are deliberately avoided here since pagan nations in ancient times deified them and worshiped them under those names. The author of Genesis wants his readers to

understand that the lights are light-bearers to be appreciated, not gods to be feared. In fact, it is the one true God
who made them (see 1:16; see also Isa. 40:26). The stars
are mentioned here almost as an afterthought, probably
because of the emphasis on the specific functions of the
sun and moon. Psalm 136:9, however, notes that the stars
help the moon "govern the night." Genesis 1:17,18 lists
the three main duties of the lights in the sky: (1) to give
light, (2) to govern day and night, and (3) to separate light
from darkness.

Day 5: Variety and quantity are stressed in the verses
encompassing days 5 and 6 (see also Ps. 104:25). Land,
sea and air were to be filled with God's creatures.

The Hebrew word underlying the phrase "creatures of
the sea" (Gen. 1:21) was used in Canaanite mythology as
the name of a dreaded sea monster who is often referred to
in a literary and figurative way in Old Testament poetry as
one of God's most powerful adversaries, whether natural
(see Job 7:12), national (Babylon: see Jer. 51:34; Egypt:
Isa. 51:9; Ezek. 29:3; 32:2), or cosmic (see Ps. 74:13; Isa.
27:1). But in Genesis he is simply the first specimen of
animate life created by God—not to be feared as an evil
enemy, but to be appreciated because God created him as
"good" (see also Ps. 148:7).

The term "winged bird" (Gen. 1:21) denotes anything
that flies, including insects (see Deut. 14:19,20).

God showed gracious loving concern to the animals
by blessing them and making it possible for them to "be
fruitful and increase in number" (Gen. 1:22). He later
gave mankind the same command and privilege, both at
the time of their creation (see 1:28) and after the Flood
(see 9:1,7).

Day 6: As we noted at 1:1, God is both a plurality and

a unity. After God said, "Let us make man in our image" (1:26), He then went on to create man "in his own image" (1:27). Though a mystery, the uni-plurality of God's nature is taught consistently throughout Scripture.

No distinction should be made between *image* and *likeness,* which are in apposition in 1:26 and are synonyms in both the Old Testament (see Gen. 5:1; 9:6) and New (see 1 Cor. 11:7; Col. 3:10; Jas. 3:9). Since we are made in God's image, every human being is worthy of honor and respect; he is to be neither murdered (see Gen. 9:6) nor cursed (see Jas. 3:9,10). Just as a coin is stamped with a ruler's image and represents his presence and authority in his realm, so we are all stamped with God's image and should therefore not only represent Him faithfully but also acknowledge His dominion over our lives. *Image* should be understood primarily in a spiritual sense here, including such qualities as "knowledge" (Col. 3:10), "righteousness and holiness" (Eph. 4:24). We who believe in Jesus are to be "conformed to the likeness" of Christ (Rom. 8:29), and some day we will be "like him" (1 John 3:2).

Genesis 1 represents man as the climax of God's creative activity. God has "crowned him with glory and honor" and "made him ruler" (Ps. 8:5-8) over the rest of His creation (see Gen. 1:26). Man is a product of divine creation (see Gen. 2:7), not of natural evolution.

Genesis 1:27 is by any standard one of the most beautiful verses in the Bible. It is the first bit of poetry in the Old Testament, which is composed of about 40 percent poetry and 60 percent prose. The distinctive verb *created* is used three times in this one verse to describe the central divine act of the sixth day. The phrase "male and female" demonstrates that both sexes were present from the beginning, although the man was created first (see Gen. 2:22; 1 Cor. 11:8; 1 Tim. 2:13). Matthew 19:4 and Mark 10:6 quote part of this verse.

One of the blessings promised in Genesis 1:28 is the begetting of children, who constitute one of God's greatest gifts to us (see Ps. 127:3-5). Another blessing is that of subduing the earth, which has to do with gaining mastery of it and its secrets rather than exploiting or polluting it.

According to Genesis 1:29,30, both people and animals were apparently vegetarian before the Flood (see 9:3).

The final verse in Genesis 1 declares all of the divine acts of creation to be "very good" indeed. All that is good has our God as its source: "Every good and perfect gift is from above, coming down from the Father of the heavenly lights" (Jas. 1:17).

Conclusion (Gen. 2:1-3)

Ancient Near Eastern literature, particularly from Mesopotamia and Canaan, provides numerous examples of the use of seven days as a literary framework to circumscribe the completion of a significant or catastrophic event. The pattern in these works runs uniformly as follows: "One day, a second day, so and so happens; a third day, a fourth day, such and such occurs; a fifth day, a sixth day, so and so takes place; then, on the seventh day, the story comes to its exciting conclusion."[3]

Genesis 1:1—2:3 exhibits a subtle and highly sophisticated modification of that literary device. While the extra-biblical poems tell their stories in terms of three sets of two days apiece followed by a seventh climactic day, the Genesis 1 Creation account uses two sets of three days apiece, each set having its own preliminary climax, the whole narrative then concluding with a majestic and extended climactic paragraph describing the seventh day. Genesis 1:1—2:3 can be sketched as follows: "On days one, two and three God gives form to the universe; on days four, five and six God fills the universe; then, on the seventh day the Creator of the universe rests from all His work."

As God "rested from all his work" (2:2), so also those of us who believe in Christ can share in the rest that Jesus provides (see Heb. 4:4,10). Biblical teaching concerning the Sabbath day finds its source ultimately in Genesis 2:1-3. Although the word *Sabbath* does not appear in Genesis 2, the Hebrew word underlying the verb *rested* (2:2,3) is the verbal form of the noun *Sabbath*. Genesis 2:3 tells us that "God blessed the seventh day and made it holy, because on it he rested." Exodus 20:8-11, after reminding the Israelites that they were to work six days and rest on the seventh because that is what God did, made the connection between the seventh day and the Sabbath day explicit by slightly paraphrasing Genesis 2:3: "Therefore the LORD blessed the Sabbath day and made it holy" (Exod. 20:11).

God did not rest until He had "finished" the work He had been doing (Gen. 2:2). In a similar way, Jesus did God's work faithfully (see John 9:4) and urged others to do the same while there was still time. And even as He was being crucified for your sins and mine, only when He was absolutely certain that His work of redemption was complete did He say these words in the hearing of all who were at the foot of His cross: "It is finished" (John 19:30).

Notes

1. B. Bavink, *The Natural Sciences* (New York: The Century Company, 1932), p. 219.

2. For additional details see R. Youngblood, "Moses and the King of Siam," *Journal of the Evangelical Theological Society* 16/4 (Fall, 1973), pp. 215-222.

3. For examples see E.A. Speiser in *Ancient Near Eastern Texts Relating to the Old Testament;* 2nd ed. J.B. Pritchard, ed. (Princeton: Princeton University Press, 1955), p. 94; H.L. Ginsberg in *Ancient Near Eastern Texts*, pp. 134,144,150.

3
CREATION II
Genesis 2:4-25

As we pointed out at the beginning of the previous chapter, the Genesis account of creation is set forth in two parts. In Genesis 1:1—2:3, man is the culmination of creation, the climax of the divine creative activity, the crowning achievement of God's work. In Genesis 2:4-25, however, the author focuses his attention on man right at the outset, so that man occupies center stage in the drama of creation.

Man Is Formed (Gen. 2:4-7)

Genesis 1:1—2:3, we remind ourselves, serves as an introduction to the primeval history (1:1—11:26). In a broader sense, of course, it provides an introduction for the entire book of Genesis.

Genesis 2:4, on the other hand, leads us into the first of the five main sections of the primeval history, "the account of the heavens and the earth." The sight of that familiar phrase, "the heavens and the earth," informs us that we are about to read another narrative about creation.

And that impression is confirmed when we look at the complete title for the section: "This is the account of the heavens and the earth when they were created."

But what a different account it is when compared to the Creation story in 1:1—2:3! The first account has a lofty dignity about it, while the second is much more simple and down-to-earth. The first narrative has stylized expressions and repeated formulas, while the second is lively and full of surprises. The first has the measured cadences of a liturgical hymn, while the second builds to an unexpected but happy climax. In the first story God is the transcendent and all-powerful Creator, while in the second "the LORD God" is closely and intimately involved in the life and experiences of the people He has created.

It will be observed that these differences do not amount to contradictions in any sense of the word. They are simply differences of emphasis or perspective. The two accounts look at the same or similar series of events from two distinctive points of view. The one is concerned with the big picture, the other with a few tantalizing details; the one sees the entire forest, the other a few trees.

Even the name of God in the two accounts is different. The supreme Being is uniformly called "God" in Genesis 1:1—2:3, the word itself being used a total of 35 times. Thirty-five equals five times seven, and the number seven plays a prominent role in the first Creation narrative. Creation is portrayed as taking place in six days followed by a seventh day of rest, as we have already seen. But it is also instructive to note that Genesis 1:1 contains exactly seven words in the original Hebrew text and that 1:2 contains exactly 14 Hebrew words (two times seven). Other similar examples could easily be pointed out and would serve to show that the author was using the number seven in its symbolic sense of completion or perfection.[1]

But symbolic numbers are not immediately apparent in 2:4-25, and the name of the supreme Being is " the LORD God" throughout the story. "LORD" is the personal, intimate name of God in the Old Testament and stresses His work as Redeemer. "God," on the other hand, is His more formal and impersonal name and emphasizes His work as Creator. Both are names of one and the same God, of course, and the compound name "LORD God" in 2:4-25 is intended to demonstrate that the formal God who creates man in the first creation account is identical to the personal LORD who communes with man in the second account. God and LORD are the two most common names for God in the Old Testament, and each of them is found thousands of times there.

That Genesis 2:4-25 zeroes in on a small area of the earth's surface is clear at the very beginning of the story. We are told that certain kinds of vegetation (called simply "field shrub" and "field plant") did not yet exist because there were no people to work the land and there was no rain to water it (see 2:5). The statement that God "had not sent rain on the earth" does not have to be understood in universal terms, because the word translated *earth* often means *land* in the sense of a local geographic region. The reference to the absence of rain, then, probably pertains to the special climate around the Garden of Eden.[2] In any event there were other sources of water available in the form of "streams" coming up from the ground. (The word *streams* was translated *mist* in the older English versions, but increased understanding of the languages of ancient Mesopotamia, from which this word ultimately comes, makes it clear that *streams* is a more accurate rendering.)

The prose description of the creation of man in 2:7,

though quite different from the poetic description in 1:27, is equally powerful in its own way. While 1:27 says that God "created" man, 2:7 states that God "formed" man. Since the two verses depict the same divine activity, it is proper to conclude that *create* and *form* are synonyms. God may create *ex nihilo* ("out of nothing") as He surely did in 1:1. But He may also create by making use of already-existing material as He did when He formed man "from the dust of the ground" (2:7). The verb *form* is used specifically of the work of a potter (see especially Isa. 45:9).

In the Hebrew text of Genesis 2:7 there is a beautiful play on words: "God formed man [*ādām*] from the dust of the ground [*ădāmāh*]." The pun reminds us that our origins are earthly. As Paul puts it: "The first man was of the dust of the earth," an "earthly man" (1 Cor. 15:47,48). But the Hebrew word *ādām* can also be read as the proper name Adam, and in ambiguous cases we must let the context decide between generic *man* and specific *Adam*. Paul's citation of the last clause of Genesis 2:7 combines the two possibilities: "The first man Adam became a living being" (1 Cor. 15:45).

Genesis 2:7 teaches that man's nature is both physical and spiritual. God not only "formed man from the dust of the ground"; He also "breathed into his nostrils the breath of life." It was only when this twofold act had been accomplished that "man became a living being." The term *living being* has nothing to do with the ancient Greek concept of a soul inhabiting a body; it is a translation of the same Hebrew phrase that is rendered "living creatures" in 1:20. Hebrew psychology knew nothing of dividing human personality into various parts or compartments. It was remarkably modern in its unified approach to what constitutes a life that is truly human.

Elihu, the young upstart in the book of Job, nevertheless provides a fine commentary on Genesis 2:7 when he says to Job, "I am just like you before God; I too have been taken from clay" (Job 33:6), and especially when he says this to Job two verses earlier: "The Spirit of God has made me; the breath of the Almighty gives me life" (33:4). Since it is God's breath and Spirit that gives us life, if He were to withdraw His life-giving power from us "all mankind would perish together and man would return to the dust" (Job 34:15; see also Ps. 104:29; Eccles. 12:7). Apart from God, says the patriarch Abraham, we are "nothing but dust and ashes" (Gen. 18:27). From a strictly financial standpoint and without the energizing power of God, the chemicals in the average human body are worth a mere $7.28 as these words are being written—even in a highly inflationary economy!

No doubt about it, Elihu was right. Though the breath of God can produce ice (see Job 37:10) or set a fire pit ablaze (see Isa. 30:33), it also can—and does—give us life. To the Lord and to Him alone, we owe our very life and breath (Acts 17:25). In Him and in Him alone, "we live and move and have our being" (17:28).

The Garden of Eden (Gen. 2:8-17)

The place that God prepared for the first man to live in must have been exquisitely beautiful. Its very name, *Eden*, is synonymous with *paradise*. The original meaning of the word is lost in obscurity. It may have been related to a Hebrew word denoting *bliss* or *delight*, or it might have come from a Mesopotamian word that means simply *a plain*. In any event, it was in Eden that God planted a garden where man was to make his first home.

Where was the Garden of Eden located? Genesis 2:8 states that it was "in the east" from the standpoint of the author. Nearly a century ago "Chinese" Gordon, the great British general who was also a devout Bible scholar, made the radical claim that the Garden of Eden was located on one of about a hundred islands in the Indian Ocean just below the equator. Known as the Seychelles, their climate is ideal and their beauty defies comparison. More specifically, Gordon pinpointed the location of the garden in the valley of Mai on Praslin island. As one British official stated a few years ago, "Whether 'Chinese' Gordon was right or wrong, you must admit that Eden *should* have been here!"³

But Gordon was surely wrong in this case, because Genesis 2:14 mentions the Tigris and Euphrates rivers in connection with Eden. This means that the garden must have been somewhere in the land known today as Iraq. While we cannot be absolutely certain about the exact site, the traditional location is in southern Iraq at the confluence of the Tigris and Euphrates. A tree stump in the area displays a plaque designating the spot as the home of Adam.

In later generations Eden became proverbial for its beauty and fertility. It is called the "garden of the LORD" in Genesis 13:10 and Isaiah 51:3 and the "garden of God" in Ezekiel 28:13; 31:9. Like most things characterized by spectacular beauty, it had the potential for good and for evil.

All kinds of magnificent trees bearing delicious fruit grew in the garden, including the "tree of life" and the "tree of the knowledge of good and evil." The tree of life is obviously desirable in every respect. In the book of Revelation, for example, the Lord says to believers in the church at Ephesus, "To him who overcomes, I will give the right to eat from the tree of life, which is in the paradise of God" (Rev. 2:7). Later in the same book the tree is mentioned again several times, its leaves and fruit being granted to the righteous (see 22:2,14) but withheld from the unrighteous (see 22:19).

And what of the tree of the knowledge of good and evil? For now, we would simply note that its very name is sinister, leaving open the possibility of either good or evil effects on anyone who eats its fruit. The fact of the matter is, however, that God Himself predicts only *one* result for the eater, and that an irreversibly final one: death (see Gen. 2:17; 3:3). A few scholars have felt, therefore, that the tree of the knowledge of good and evil could just as appropriately have been called the tree of death. The two most crucial trees in the garden would then have been the tree of life, bringing life to its eaters, and the tree of death, resulting in death for its eaters.

It is very intriguing, therefore, that a few years ago a Canaanite religious text was discovered in Syria that clearly refers to a "tree of death."[4] This is the only known mention of such a tree in ancient Near Eastern literature. So it is possible that *tree of death* was an alternate name for the tree of the knowledge of good and evil in ancient Israelite tradition outside of the Bible. But even if that should prove to be so, the biblical name is far superior for the purposes of the author of Genesis, as we shall soon see.

Returning now to the Garden of Eden, we note that in addition to the Tigris and Euphrates two other rivers are mentioned in connection with it: the Pishon (which winds through the land of Havilah), and the Gihon (which winds through the land of Cush). It is theoretically possible to translate *Pishon* and *Gihon* as common nouns (*gusher* and *spurter,* or the like) and so avoid the necessity of identifying them with known rivers. But since *Tigris* and *Euphrates* are proper nouns it is quite likely that *Pishon* and *Gihon* are also. Up to the present time they have not been located, although they would have had to be situated somewhere in southeastern Mesopotamia. As to Havilah and Cush, we know that there was a Cush in Mesopotamia during the days of Nimrod, the ruler of Babylon, Erech and other important cities in that region (see Gen. 10:8-12). So even though Cush usually means *northern Sudan* "called *Ethiopia* in ancient times" in the Old Testament, it cannot mean that in 2:13 because of the great distance between Africa and Mesopotamia (modern Iraq). There are two areas called *Havilah* in the Bible (the first is mentioned in 10:7, the second in 10:29; it is doubtless the latter Havilah that was in or near the Garden of Eden).

The Tigris and Euphrates are the two mightiest rivers in Mesopotamia, and in fact gave the region its name (Mesopotamia means simply "between the [two] rivers"). Both are indeed "great" rivers (see Gen. 15:18; Dan. 10:4), and the Euphrates is often called "the River" (1 Kings 4:21,24) *par excellence*.

The Search for a Helper (Gen. 2:18-20)

Fellowship, friendship and intimacy are basic needs of every human being, implanted in us by God Himself: "It is not good for the man to be alone" (2:18). But although animals and man both came from "the ground" (2:7; 2:19), animals can never provide for man the kind and degree of companionship he really requires. Man's helper must be "suitable for him" (2:18).

To allow Adam to see this for himself, God brought

all the animals to Adam "to see what he would name them" (2:19). As Adam gave each animal a name he thereby demonstrated that he was in control of them, that he was their master (see also 2 Kings 23:34; 24:17). In so doing he began to fulfill God's command given to him earlier: "Rule over" them (Gen. 1:28; see also 1:26).

The name of Adam himself has often been identified with the name *Adapa,* found in a number of Mesopotamian texts. Such an identification is now unnecessary, however, because two years ago the word *Adam* was found in a cuneiform text from Ebla in northern Syria. It appears in that text as a personal name and is the first such occurrence outside the Bible. This discovery strengthens considerably the traditional view that the biblical Adam was a real person and not simply a personification of mankind in general.

Woman is Made (Gen. 2:21-25)

Since none of the animals provided a suitable helper for Adam, God proceeded to make one for him. Genesis 2:21 describes the first case of controlled anesthesia in history! While Adam was sleeping, God took one of the man's ribs and made a woman from it.

In Sumerian, one of the languages of Mesopotamia, the word for *rib* also means *life.* Something of that concept is also intended here: The woman comes into being out of the very life of the man. Life begets life.

But surely much more is intended here as well. As many commentators have noted, the woman was not made from one of the bones in the man's head in order to make it possible for her to lord it over him, nor was she made from one of the bones in his foot in order to enable him to trample and crush her. On the contrary, she was made from one of the bones in his side, so that they might share life together in mutual protection and concern and love and care.[5] It is only sin that changed that original divine intention (see Gen. 3:16) and brought about man's subjugation of woman in ways that are often cruel and unjust.

But how perfect was that original pristine relationship! Adam expressed his unbounded delight in the Bible's second poem:

> "This is now bone of my bones
> and flesh of my flesh;
> she shall be called 'woman,'
> for she was taken out of man."

As in English, so also in Hebrew the words for *man* and *woman* sound very much alike. Even in themselves they serve to help cement the one-flesh union—monogamy, not polygamy—that was the divine intention for husbands and wives from the beginning. One man would be united to one woman, and they would become one flesh (see Gen. 2:24) forever (see Matt. 19:4-6). And in that primeval state of innocence, their nakedness would cause them no shame.

Notes

1. See U. Cassuto, *A Commentary on the Book of Genesis, Part I: From Adam to Noah* (Jerusalem: Magnes Press, 1961), pp. 13-15.
2. G.L. Archer, *Decision* (February, 1973), p. 5.
3. G. Gaskill, "Armchair Voyage to Paradise," *Reader's Digest* (August, 1961), pp. 139,140.
4. M. Tsevat, "The Two Trees in the Garden of Eden" (paper read at the Society of Biblical Literature annual meeting, November 9, 1973).
5. W.H. Griffith Thomas, *Genesis: A Devotional Commentary* (Grand Rapids: Eerdmans Publishing Company, 1946), p. 43.

4

CREATION: LATE OR EARLY?

Genesis 1:1—2:25

When did creation take place? How old is the universe? Was the earth created at the same time the universe came into being? When was life created? How long ago did God make the first man?

Until about two centuries ago, Jewish and Christian scholars alike turned to the pages of the Old Testament in their search for answers to such questions. They agreed almost unanimously that all of creation took place about six thousand years ago in six 24-hour days. Using various genealogies and other chronological references in the Old Testament, James Ussher (1581-1656), archbishop of Armagh in northern Ireland, placed the date of creation more specifically in the year 4004 B.C. His contemporary, the Hebraist John Lightfoot (1602-1675), agreed with him and determined that the Creation week was October 18-23 and that Adam was created on the sixth day of that week at nine o'clock in the morning, forty-fifth meridian time.

Although such attempts at precision are no longer taken seriously, the basic view that creation is relatively late and that it occurred a few tens of thousands of years ago (at the very most) is still held by many students of Scripture—and for understandable reasons. After all, it seems to represent what the text of the Bible actually says, at least when interpreted literally. It also seems to dovetail best with the biblical concept of an all-powerful God, who "spoke, and it came to be" (Ps. 33:9).

In spite of these arguments and others, however, the *late-earth theory* is in the distinct minority in today's scholarly community—even among Christian men and women of science (among, for example, the members of the American Scientific Affiliation, an association of evangelical scientists of national distinction and international reputation). In fact, it is virtually the unanimous viewpoint of competent scientists that astronomy and astrophysics have successfully demonstrated the universe to be tens of billions of years old, that geology and paleontology have conclusively shown the earth and the earliest forms of life to be billions of years old, and that paleoanthropology and archaeology have proved beyond doubt that hominids (manlike creatures, though not necessarily human beings in the biblical sense) have been on the earth for millions of years.

Needless to say, proponents of the *early-earth theory* do not agree with each other in detail any more than the late-earth theorists agree among themselves. Estimates change as new evidence accumulates and as new methods of evaluating that evidence are developed. But the following approximate figures represent the current consensus:

> Universe—14.5 billion years old
> Earth—4.6 billion years old[1]
> Life—3.8 billion years old[2]
> Hominids—5.0 million years old[3]

(Man in the biblical sense is doubtless much more recent, as we shall attempt to show later in this chapter.) These figures are derived not from only one system of measurement or calculation but from numerous converging lines of evidence resulting in similar conclusions arrived at independently of each other. One author has this to say in a discussion of a particular group of measurement methods: "To get a value of 6,000 years for the age of the earth one would have to assume an error of 99.9998 percent for *each of the major radioactive methods*. Inasmuch as the different methods employ different techniques and . . . different assumptions, an error of such magnitude as this is quite incredible."[4]

In any event, the strong possibility that the early-earth theory is substantially correct forces us to take a closer look at the Genesis account of Creation. Since the works of God (as revealed in nature) and the Word of God (the Bible) do not conflict when each is properly understood, and since the early-earth theory gets much the better of the argument over the late-earth theory in terms of hard scientific data, perhaps the historical narratives of Genesis 1—11 should be understood in something other than the traditional sense. Once scientific facts have been established as precisely as is humanly possible, "the redemptive thinker will . . . strive to interpret the biblical revelation in a way which is consistent with scientific truth."[5] And since the Bible is undeniably the finest and greatest piece of literature ever penned, we would agree that "the language of the Bible is more like the language of literature than that of science."[6]

The late-earth theory is based primarily on (1) a literal interpretation of the "days" of Genesis 1, (2) a literal interpretation of the genealogies of Genesis 5 and 11 (often also including an insistence that there are no gaps in them), and (3) a rereading of selective scientific data to harmonize with said literal interpretation. We wish to discuss here the nature of the "days" of Genesis 1, leaving for chapter 7 our treatment of the genealogies.

The "Days" of Genesis 1

The necessity of a literal interpretation of the word *day* in the first chapter of Genesis is more apparent than real, since there have been dissenting voices throughout the history of the church. Augustine, for example, referred to the days of Creation as "ineffable," believing that 24-hour days were unworthy of an omnipotent God and considering the word *day* to be a figure of speech in Genesis 1. In this connection we do well to remind ourselves that the omnipotence of God is not the point at issue here, because the task of the interpreter is not to try to discover what God *could* do, since a sovereign and all-powerful God "does whatever pleases him" (Ps. 115:3). It is rather the interpreter's task to find out, if possible, what God *did in fact* do, and that can be learned only through painstaking and patient study of the inspired Scriptures coupled with a teachable willingness to give up our earlier ideas, no matter how deeply cherished or long held.

A careful examination of the use of *day* in Genesis 1:1—2:3 indicates that the word means at least three different things in that passage: (1) 12 hours in 1:5,14,16,18; (2) 24 hours in 1:5,8,13,14,19,23,31; (3) an unspecified length of time in 2:2,3. So it is clear that it need not be interpreted literally in the first part of the Creation narrative even by the standards of Genesis itself.

But what about that sixth day—the day on which man and woman were created? Genesis 2:4-25, we have argued (we believe correctly so), tells essentially the same story as does Genesis 1:1—2:3 but focuses on a restricted area of the earth's surface (Eden). Allowing for the instantaneous creation of the land animals, man and woman, we must nevertheless take note also of Adam's activity on the sixth day. During the time between his creation and Eve's, God (1) put him in the garden "to work it and take care of it"; (2) gave him a command with respect to the trees in the garden; (3) brought "all the beasts of the field and all the birds of the air" (hundreds—or thousands—of different "kinds"?) to see what he would name them, a monumental task that Adam successfully undertook (by no means a casual procedure, naming was a serious matter that was done carefully and thoughtfully in ancient times); and (4) observed that Adam had gradually realized that none of the birds or animals was a "suitable helper" for him and that he had had time to become lonely (as reflected in Adam's joyful exclamation in 2:23). That all of this took place within 24 hours is impossible to believe.

Finally, what about the seventh day—the day on which God "rested from all his work"? Christian theology has traditionally taught that God's rest from His initial creative activity is still in effect and will continue forever. The seventh day, then, is everlasting.

It would seem that Augustine was right all along: Genesis tells us nothing about the time span of creation. The days are literary and timeless, not literal and time-bound. This understanding of the days lends further support to our interpretation of Genesis 1:1—2:3 as given in chapter 2. At the same time it has negative implications for competing interpretations, to a sampling of which we now turn.

Other Views of Genesis 1:1—2:3

The gap theory: Those who hold this position teach that a perfect creation (see 1:1) was followed by a universal catastrophe that destroyed it (see 1:2; or between 1:1 and 1:2) and that in turn was followed by a perfect re-creation (see 1:3-31). The gap between 1:1 and 1:2 (or between 1:1 and 1:3) gives sufficient "scope for all the geologic ages."[7] Geology needs time, and the gap theory provides it—billions of years if necessary.

While the gap theory has been attacked from many different angles, it has one especially fatal flaw: It cannot stand up to the statement in Exodus 20:11 that "in six days the LORD made the heavens and the earth." In other words, "the heavens and the earth" of Genesis 1:1 were created during the six days, not prior to an indefinite period of time before the days began.

The geologic-era theory: Proponents of this view hold that the *days* of Genesis 1 are not to be understood as literal 24-hour days but are to be interpreted metaphorically as geologic eras or ages. They are days from God's standpoint, since "with the Lord a day is like a thousand years, and a thousand years are like a day" (2 Pet. 3:8). Many late nineteenth- and early twentieth-century geologists within the church taught and popularized this theory.

But geologic ages tend to overlap with each other and are not capable of the sort of rigid division implied by the words, "And there was evening, and there was morning— the first day" (Gen. 1:5; see also 1:8,13,19,23,31). And while it is true that the Hebrew word for *day* is somewhat elastic, we should probably not press it to denote so lengthy a period as a geologic era.

Progressive creationism: This view inserts periods of millions or billions of years between the days of Genesis 1 and assumes that God's creative activity took place in a series of steps separated by eons. In so doing, it tries to preserve the advantages of the traditional interpretation of 24-hour days on the one hand and those of the geologic-era theory on the other. An approach that bears at least an oblique relationship to this view is that of *threshold evolution,* which teaches that Genesis 1 neither affirms nor denies the possibility of biological evolution within the kinds but that these great divisions of the plant and animal kingdoms cannot be violated by the evolutionary process since each had to be created separately by God.

But although progressive creationism has undoubted strengths it has its weaknesses as well. The gap theory assumes one gap; progressive creationism must assume several gaps and, in so doing, multiplies the difficulty. Also, while it preserves the advantages of the 24-hour day and geologic-era theories, it combines or compounds their disadvantages at the same time, so that nothing is gained in the process.

It will be observed that all of these theories, and many others like them, tend to view the days of Genesis 1 as time-bound, as related to time in some way. But as we tried to show earlier, the use of "day" in 1:1—2:3 is by no means uniform. For that and other literary reasons, it is best to consider the days as indefinite and timeless.

In any event, however, both Genesis and geology place the emergence of man at the very end of the sequence of events. Science tells us that manlike creatures began to appear on the earth at least five million years ago.

But the biblical account as related in Genesis 1:26—11:26 cannot be interpreted to allow for the creation of Adam that far back in time. Does that mean, then, that the estimates of science are wrong in this case?

Not necessarily.

Early Earth, Late Man

Genesis 1:27 states that man was created "in the image of God." Genesis 2:7 adds that God "formed man from the dust of the ground and breathed into his nostrils the breath of life" and that "man became a living being." These descriptions of the origin of biblical man indicate that God did something highly extraordinary at the end of the Creation sequence. By a special act of creation, God made men from dust and in the divine image. Whatever hominids (Cro-Magnon, Neanderthal, and earlier) may have existed prior to the time of Adam, they had only animal intelligence and were not bound to God in a covenant relationship.

Recent prolonged studies of various primates have shown that they possess remarkable intelligence and ingenuity, as well as a rudimentary creativity. Even in the wild they make tools from twigs to obtain food, greet one another with kisses and embraces, show off when old and mimic when young. In captivity they can be trained to communicate in various ways. A gorilla named Koko, for example, has been taught 300 signs of the American sign language (a system of communication routinely used by the deaf). Lana, a chimpanzee, has mastered a vocabulary of a hundred words formed by pressing, in predetermined order, combinations of colored keys bearing nine geometrical symbols on a computer keyboard. With it she composes grammatically correct sentences that answer researchers' questions or make requests for treats. Perhaps most amazing of all, another chimpanzee, named Moja, drew a simple design with chalk on a blackboard and, when asked what it was, made the American sign language sign for "bird."[8]

If primates can demonstrate such a degree of brainpower, it should not surprise us that pre-Adamic hominids had similar skills. Six hundred carefully fashioned knifelike tools, unearthed in the last decade and used by early hominids, have been firmly dated at 2.6 million years old.[9] An engraved bone 135,000 years old was excavated several years ago in the rich archaeological region of the Dordogne in France. Called the oldest "work of art" yet discovered, it is a complex expressive form carved by a pre-Neanderthal hominid.[10]

Such skills and capacities in these pre-Adamic creatures, however, are proof neither of humanity in the biblical sense nor of moral and spiritual sensitivity. Adam and Eve, the first "man" and "woman" in the biblical sense of those terms, date back to a few tens of thousands of years ago at best. Scientists are free to date pre-Adamic hominids to much earlier periods.[11] Compared to such hominids who were part of the early earth, biblical man is relatively late in time. And we are all the spiritual descendants of the biblical Adam himself, through whom "sin entered the world" (Rom. 5:12).

What Genesis 1:1—2:25 Teaches Us About Creation

Although the first two chapters of Genesis do in fact speak volumes to the scientist, their main interest is theological. They are more concerned with the who and why than they are with the how and when. They give us "a doctrine of a Creator rather than a doctrine of creation."[12]

They introduce us to God and to man and to God's relationship with man. Here are a few of their major teachings:

God is outside the universe and above it as its Creator. Against materialism, which teaches that matter is everything and eternal, Genesis teaches that God is eternal, above matter, and the Creator of matter (which is therefore neither eternal nor everything). Against pantheism, which teaches that everything is God or that God is in everything, Genesis teaches that God is separate from His creation and above it. Against dualism, which teaches that a struggle rages between two equally matched gods or principles, one evil and the other good, Genesis assumes the existence of one good God who declares each of His creative works to be "good" and stamps the whole creative sequence "very good." Against polytheism, which teaches that there are many gods who are often at odds with each other, Genesis teaches that there is only one beneficent God.

God created all the denizens of the universe. He both formed it and filled it: "The earth is the LORD's, and everything in it, the world, and all who live in it" (Ps. 24:1). God even made those beings and things whom man called God's enemies: "the deep," denied divine status and equated with "the waters" (1:2); "the great creatures of the sea," created by His mighty hand and pronounced "good" (1:21); "two great lights" and "the stars" (1:16), God's celestial rivals whom people often worshiped in preference to Him; and animals of all kinds, God's creatures great and small, to be effectively controlled by man rather than deified by him.

God made man as the crown and climax of His creative activity, as His highest and finest creation, as the particular object of His special providence and care. Everything else was made in a beautiful and orderly pattern, each in its time being prepared for eventual dominion by man.

Man was created as totally distinct from the animals. He was not to mate with them, worship them, or relate himself in any other degrading way to them. On the contrary, he was to exercise lordship over them and make them his servants.

Man found his only suitable counterpart in woman, who together became the physical and spiritual progenitors of the entire human family.

> O Lord my God, when I in awesome wonder
> Consider all the worlds
>   thy hands have made,
> I see the stars, I hear the rolling thunder,
> Thy power throughout
>   the universe displayed,
>
> Then sings my soul, my Savior God, to thee,
>   "How great thou art! How great thou art!"
> —Stuart K. Hine

Notes

1. *Newsweek* magazine (April 19, 1976), p. 10.
2. *Newsweek* magazine (August 6, 1979), p. 77; *Newsweek* (June 30, 1980), p. 61.
3. *Newsweek* magazine (May 21, 1979), pp. 59,60.
4. D. England, *A Christian View of Origins* (Grand Rapids: Baker Book House, 1972), p. 105.
5. C.S. Evans, *Preserving the Person* (Downers Grove, IL: Inter-Varsity Press, 1977), p. 142.
6. A.F. Holmes, *All Truth Is God's Truth* (Grand Rapids: William B.

Eerdmans Publishing Company, 1977), p. 47.

7. *The Scofield Reference Bible* (New York: Oxford University Press, 1909), p. 3, n. 2.

8. *Newsweek* magazine (March 7, 1977), pp. 70-73.

9. *Newsweek* magazine (December 24, 1973), p. 102.

10. *Newsweek* magazine (December 18, 1972), p. 70.

11. G.L. Archer in *Decision* magazine (February, 1973), p. 5, and in *Decision* magazine (February, 1980), p. 14.

12. D.F. Payne, *Genesis One Reconsidered* (London: The Tyndale Press, 1964), p. 23.

5
THE FALL

Genesis 3:1-24

The other day a friend, with justifiable pride, showed me a snapshot of a beautiful little girl: her two-month-old niece. After doing the appropriate (and in this case spontaneous) oohing and aahing, I said to my friend, "Wouldn't it be a wonderful thing if everyone in the world stayed as innocent and lovable and trusting as your little niece is right now? What a paradise this world would be!"

She agreed, of course—and then both of us quickly returned to the harsh realities of our workaday situations, knowing full well that even in the best of circumstances our lives are beset with problems and difficulties and heartaches and pain and grief, and that all of these can be traced ultimately to the most basic evil in the world: human sin.

And my friend and I also realized—sadly, to be sure—that her niece has been a "sinner from birth," just as the psalmist confessed of himself (see Ps. 51:5). We knew that as she grew into childhood and then womanhood her life would increasingly demonstrate her fundamentally sinful nature in a number of different ways. We knew that even this lovely little baby girl was by no means exempt from the verdict laid down long ago by the apostle Paul: "All have sinned" (Rom. 3:23).

Where did this awful thing known as "sin" come from? What is its origin?

Genesis 3 gives us a vivid picture of how sin entered the world, a picture that we shall examine in detail. We would observe in passing, however, that even a chapter describing the fall of man into sin can bear the marks of a literary craftsman of the first order. The ebb and flow of the events outlined in Genesis 3 have a striking symmetry all their own: (1) The serpent sins (3:1-5), then the woman, and finally the man (3:6); (2) the Lord then confronts them with their sin by speaking to them in the reverse order: first the man (3:9-12), then the woman (3:13), and finally the serpent (3:14); (3) the Lord concludes this phase of His response to them by judging them in the same order in which they had sinned: first the serpent (3:14,15), next the woman (3:16), and last of all the man (3:17-19). The chapter ends with one of the saddest scenes in all of Scripture: The Lord banishes the man and his wife from the Garden of Eden (3:22-24), where He had originally put him (see 2:8).

Having briefly analyzed the literary structure of the chapter, we now turn to a topical discussion of what Genesis 3 teaches us about the fall of man into sin.

The Test

It was just as true back then as it is now: God may test us, but He never tempts us. James 1:13 tells us that God does not "tempt anyone."

Testing and tempting may be distinguished from each other in two ways. First, the subject of testing is always God (ultimately), while the subject of tempting is always Satan (ultimately). It is Satan who tempts; God never tempts anyone.

Second, the objects or purposes of testing and tempting differ from each other. The object of temptation is the fall of the person being tempted. When Satan tempts us he hopes that we will fall into sin. But that is not true of testing. The purpose of tempting is to make us *worse,* while the purpose of testing is to make us *better.*

Look, for example, at Deuteronomy 8:2: "God led you all the way in the desert these forty years, to humble you and to test you in order to know what was in your heart, whether or not you would keep his commands." And follow that up with 8:16: "He gave you manna to eat in the desert, . . . to humble and to test you so that in the end it might go well with you."

That is why God tests us—so that in the end it might go well with us; so that positive results might be the outcome; so that we might grow in grace and in the knowledge of Him; so that we might be better people after the period of testing is over.

And that is why God tested Adam and his wife in the Garden of Eden—to strengthen their faith and trust in Him.

Reality and Symbol

We believe that the fall of man actually took place in history and as described in Genesis 3. At the same time, the various elements in the story symbolize profound spiritual truths that are deeply meaningful to us today.[1]

One spiritual truth is that the serpent symbolizes

temptation and sin. In Revelation 20:2 (see also 12:9) he is called "that ancient serpent, who is the devil, or Satan." It is he who brought evil into the world of mankind by placing in the woman's mind doubts concerning God's providence. He said to her, "Did God really say . . . ?" (Gen. 3:1). The serpent was crafty and the woman succumbed to temptation. The suggestion to doubt God worked on her mind and heart and she fell into sin.

The apostle Paul warns us that the same thing can easily happen to us today. "I am afraid that just as Eve was deceived by the serpent's cunning, your minds may somehow be led astray from your sincere and pure devotion to Christ" (2 Cor. 11:3). None of us is immune from the clever wiles of Satan, who "prowls around like a roaring lion looking for someone to devour" (1 Pet. 5:8).

A second spiritual truth—the Garden of Eden, the most ideal and idyllic place on the face of the earth, is a symbol of fellowship with God. It was there that God "put the man he had formed" (Gen. 2:8); it was there that God gave him satisfying work to do (see 2:15); it was there that God walked "in the cool of the day" (3:8); it was there that God "made garments of skin for Adam and his wife and clothed them" (3:21).

Eviction from the garden, then, implied alienation from God and exclusion from fellowship with Him. Because of man's sin, God "banished him" from the Garden of Eden (3:23) and his relationship to God would never again be the same.

A third spiritual truth—the tree of the knowledge of good and evil plays a crucial role in Genesis 2 and 3, and as such it symbolizes the period of testing itself. God used the tree as a means of testing Adam (see 2:17), as a means of strengthening his faith and confirming his obedience.

The serpent, on the other hand, used the same tree as a means of tempting the woman (see 3:1-5), as a means of causing her to fall into sin. In allowing herself to be deceived by the serpent she disobeyed God and then caused Adam to do the same (see 3:6).

As we observed in chapter 2, the Hebrew language had no word for *universe,* and so it used the phrase "the heavens and the earth" (1:1; 2:1,4) instead. Similarly, Hebrew could not express the concepts of *moral knowledge* or *ethical discernment* apart from using the phrase "good and evil" or the like (see especially Deut. 1:39; Isa. 7:15,16). By eating the fruit of the tree of the knowledge of good and evil, Adam and his wife left the state of moral innocence in which they had been created and entered a state of moral responsibility to which God had not called them. No longer did they share a childlike faith in God; they now had reached the age of accountability, of moral adulthood. Like disobedient children, they had sinned against their loving Father.

And how clever Satan was in bringing them to such a sad and sorry state of affairs! He had told the woman that if she ate the fruit she would become "like God, knowing good and evil" (Gen. 3:5)—and in a horribly perverted sense that is exactly what happened (see 3:22). All the trees in the garden were "pleasing to the eye and good for food" (2:9), but the serpent succeeded in convincing the woman that the tree of the knowledge of good and evil had fruit that, in addition to being "good for food and pleasing to the eye," was "also desirable for gaining wisdom" (3:6).

Satan has the demonic ability of taking things that are not necessarily evil in and of themselves and twisting them for his own diabolical purposes. When he tempted

Jesus for 40 days in the desert, he took something that was potentially "good for food" and said to our Lord, "Tell this stone to become bread" (Luke 4:3). He then took something that was "pleasing to the eye" and showed Jesus "all the kingdoms of the world," promising to give Him "all their authority and splendor" (4:5,6). Finally, Satan played on the universally human desire for power and "wisdom" and dared Jesus to throw Himself down from "the highest point of the temple" (4:9). But Jesus deflected each of Satan's fiery darts and rendered them useless by quoting, each in its turn, a verse of Scripture appropriate to the temptation. In successfully defeating the devil on this and other occasions, our Lord remains to this day the only person in history "who has been tempted in every way, just as we are—yet was without sin" (Heb. 4:15).

But, totally unlike Jesus Christ, Adam and his wife failed their test miserably. While still in their innocent state they had two options available to them: they were (1) *able to sin* and (2) *able not to sin*. If they had passed their test by obeying God, He would doubtless have confirmed them in righteousness and made them *not able to sin*. It is inconceivable that God would have relentlessly put them through an endless series of tests, each one a bit harder than the previous one. Such activity might characterize an ogre, but surely not a loving heavenly Father. Adam and his wife, however, did not succeed in passing the most elementary test that God gave them. The result? They became *not able not to sin*—and that universal tendency to disobey God at every opportunity became their awful legacy to the whole human race. In its quaint but devastatingly correct way, the *New England Primer* described the human predicament as follows for generations of children in colonial America: "In Adam's fall/we sinned all."

A fourth spiritual truth—the tree of life, the garden's only other tree that is given a symbolic name in the Genesis account, exemplifies life in the full sense of that term. Life means different things to different people, of course. To take just one example, for some of us life equals wealth; but Jesus is careful to remind us that "a man's life does not consist in the abundance of his possessions" (Luke 12:15). On the contrary, life in the biblical sense is better described in qualitative than in quantitative terms. Of His followers Jesus says, "I have come that they may have life, and have it to the full" (John 10:10).

It is that kind of life that the tree of life in Genesis symbolizes. It is only that kind of life that is worth living forever, without interruption. And it is precisely that kind of life that Adam and his wife forfeited when they sinned against God. Having eaten the fruit of the tree of the knowledge of good and evil, they were no longer allowed to eat the fruit of the tree of life (see Gen. 3:22,23).

A fifth spiritual truth is that if life is symbolized by the tree of life, death is symbolized by the return to dust. When God formed man from the dust of the ground He "breathed into his nostrils the breath of life, and man became a living being" (2:7). After man sinned, the very ground from which he had been taken was cursed because of him (see 3:17), and death returned him to its dust (see 3:19). Freshly dug graves the world over still open wide their mouths, eventually to receive us all—and all because of our sinful rebellion against God. "The wages of sin is death" (Rom. 6:23).

A garden and its trees, a serpent and dust—real entities, one and all. But how familiar and vivid are the spiritual truths they symbolize! Here is how James summarizes much the same story: "Each one is tempted when, by his own evil desire, he is dragged away and enticed. Then, after desire has conceived, it gives birth to sin; and sin, when it is full-grown, gives birth to death" (Jas. 1:14,15).

Passing the Buck

Genesis 4 teaches us that the flames of sin, once kindled, spread like wildfire. Even in Genesis 3, however, the initial stages of sin's tendency to stain everything it touches stand out in bold relief.

In their state of innocence "the man and his wife were both naked, and they felt no shame" (2:25). But no sooner had they sinned than "they realized they were naked . . . and made coverings for themselves" (3:7). They even used their nakedness as an excuse to hide from God (see 3:10). What had originally been a morally neutral quality was transformed by sin into a cause for shame and fear.

And sin changes trust into fear as well. A healthy dose of remorse would have done Adam a world of good when God confronted him with his sinful deed, but Adam chose to blame it all on his wife (see 3:12). She in turn chose to blame the serpent (see 3:13). In these earliest days of man's relationship toward God, flight from responsibility quickly became a stampede.

As God asked Cain where his brother was in order to give him a chance to respond (see 4:9), so God said to Adam, "Where are you?" (3:9)—not because He could not find him, but because He wanted Adam to respond in joyful obedience.

With the same desire, God calls to us today.

Grace in the Midst of Justice

Because God is just, He must judge sin; and because God is loving, He gives grace to the sinner. It is not surprising, then, that grace and justice intermingle in each case as God judges the serpent, the woman and the man.

Though all were judged, only the serpent was cursed—and that is just. He initiated the temptation that led to human sin and his judgment is therefore the most severe. Dust, the symbol of death, would be his food and he would crawl on his belly in abject misery as long as he lived.

But he would in fact live—and there is an element of grace in all of life, however miserable. Ultimately the offspring of the woman would crush the serpent's head, and there is far greater grace in that fact.

Traditionally Genesis 3:15 has been called the *protevangelium* ("first gospel"), because already as early as the second century A.D. scholars of the caliber of Justin Martyr and Irenaeus taught that the woman's offspring referred to Christ who would some day defeat Satan himself.[2] Although the passage teaches that truth in a general way, the apostle Paul understands the whole body of believers as involved in crushing Satan (see Rom. 16:20; see 16:18,19 for evidence that Paul is reflecting on the context of Gen. 3). The church shares with her risen Lord the privilege of fulfilling the prophecy of Genesis 3:15.

Just as the serpent is cursed in what constitutes his nature as serpent, so also the woman is judged in what constitutes her nature as woman. Her labor pains would be increased in childbearing (see 3:16). In addition, however, she would now submit herself to the will of her husband, even though earlier he had submitted himself to hers (see 3:6). In all of this there is justice.

But grace shines forth as well, because the woman would "give birth to children." We think here of Carl Sandburg's definition of a baby: "God's opinion that the world should go on." Through the miracle of childbirth the human race, sinful though it is, would continue. In grateful acknowledgment of God's blessing in this regard, "Adam named his wife Eve, because she would become the mother of all the living" (3:20). The Hebrew word for *Eve* looks very much like the Hebrew word for *living*.

As in the case of the woman, so also in the case of the man: God judges him in connection with the role that characterizes him as man. He would be the breadwinner for the family but he would be forced to wrest food from the soil by the sweat of his brow (see 3:19). He would literally work himself to death and in doing so his "painful toil" (3:17) would match the pains of his wife (see 3:16).

Again, however, there are signs of grace in God's judgment on the man. He would have to work hard, to be sure; but three times God says to him, "You will eat" (3:17,18,19). The food produced by the man would sustain the lives produced by the woman, and it would sustain their own lives as well.

But perhaps there is another lesson to be learned here. If it be true that "an idle mind is the devil's workshop," if it be true that too much leisure time gives us too many opportunities for sin, then there is yet another element of grace in working long and hard.

Nevertheless, Genesis 3 ends on a somber note. Man's last and most vivid memory of the garden from which he had been driven was that of a portal flanked by cherubim, reminiscent of those awe-inspiring winged, human-headed bulls of Assyro-Babylonian sculpture that guarded the entrances to temples and palaces in ancient Mesopotamia.[3] The cherubim at Eden kept man from eating the fruit of the tree of life and served to remind him that his legacy was death caused by sin. And if he considered the cherubim his enemies, it was only because he had forgotten that his own worst enemy was himself.

Or, as the late Walt Kelly used to express it through the lips of one of his little cartoon characters in the *Pogo* comic strip:

"We have met the enemy, and he is us."

Notes

1. See especially G. Vos, *Biblical Theology* (Grand Rapids: William B. Eerdmans Publishing Company, 1948), pp. 37-51.
2. H.P. Rüger, "On Some Versions of Genesis 3.15, Ancient and Modern," in *The Bible Translator* 27/1 (January, 1976), p. 106.
3. J.D. Davis, *Genesis and Semitic Tradition* (Grand Rapids: Baker Book House, 1980 [Charles Scribner's Sons, 1894), pp. 78-84.

6
THE RAPID "PROGRESS" OF SIN

Genesis 4:1-16

Sin on a rampage—that is the main theme of the first half of Genesis 4. Once sin was unleashed in the world, there was no stopping it. Everyone on earth fell under its sinister power, and it tainted everything it touched. Following the evil example of Adam and Eve, their descendants sinned against God in open rebellion. "Since they did not think it worthwhile to retain the knowledge of God, he gave them over to a depraved mind, to do what ought not to be done. They have become filled with every kind of wickedness, evil, greed and depravity. They are full of envy, murder, strife, deceit and malice. They are gossips, slanderers, God-haters, insolent, arrogant and boastful; they invent ways of doing evil; they disobey their parents; they are senseless, faithless, heartless, ruthless" (Rom. 1:28-31).

What a frightening description—and indictment—of sinful mankind! Our earliest ancestors had the unparalleled potential of deepening their relationship with a loving heavenly Father, but they chose to exchange "the knowledge of God" (Rom. 1:28) for "the knowledge of good and evil" (Gen. 2:9,17).

Two Brothers (Gen. 4:1-7)

Knowledge and *knowing* are key terms in Genesis 3 and 4. "Knowing good and evil," Adam was driven from the Garden of Eden (3:22,23). When God asked Adam's son Cain where his brother Abel was, Cain replied, "I don't know" (4:9). And knowledge in a very special sense is the opening motif of Genesis 4.

"Adam lay with [literally, knew] his wife Eve" (4:1). The Hebrew verb *know* is almost never used in a casual sense. Far from reflecting merely knowledge by acquaintance, it nearly always refers to knowledge by experience. Unlike the former, which tends to be shallow and fleeting, biblical knowledge is deep and lasting. For that reason "to know" is often used to mean "to have sexual intercourse," the most intimate experience a husband and wife can share.

When Eve, "the mother of all the living" (3:20), had given birth to Cain she said, "With the help of the LORD I have brought forth a man" (4:1). Cain's name sounds very much like the Hebrew verb here translated as "brought forth." The same verb is used by Melchizedek in 14:19 and by Abram in 14:22 when they call God the "Creator of heaven and earth." The God who created everything that exists, the God who brought forth the heavens and the earth, helped Eve to bring forth a baby boy.

Eve's second son was named Abel, a Hebrew word that signifies a lack of permanence or meaning. The same basic word is found at the beginning and near the end of Ecclesiastes pointing to one of the major themes of that book: "Meaningless! Meaningless! . . . Everything is meaningless" (Eccles. 1:2; 12:8). In Abel's case his very name reminds us that his life itself was soon to be cut short.

The classic confrontation between the farmer and the shepherd is merely incidental in the story of Cain and Abel. The narrative focuses, rather, on the nature of the offering that each man brought to the Lord. Sacrifice, properly understood, is always the gift of life or the choicest product of one's livelihood. Much is often made of the fact that Abel's offering was an animal sacrifice while Cain's was a gift of plants, and this is sometimes connected with the supposed contrast between the "garments of skin" (Gen. 3:21) that God made for Adam and Eve and the coverings of "fig leaves" they made for themselves (3:7). It is then implied that God demands blood sacrifices and that man far too often responds with bloodless offerings.

But the Cain and Abel story stresses an entirely different matter. The issue at stake is not the nature of the offering but the heart attitude of the offerer. Cain brought "some of the fruits of the soil" (4:3) to the Lord, apparently random samples of what he had grown. Abel, on the other hand, brought "fat portions from some of the firstborn of his flock" (4:4). He cared enough to give the very best he had and so the Lord "looked with favor" on both him and his offering. But because of Cain's careless and indifferent attitude while bringing his offering, God "did not look with favor" (4:5) on either him or his gift. Unlike Cain, Abel was motivated by faith in God: "By faith Abel offered God a better sacrifice than Cain did. By faith he was commended as a righteous man, when God spoke well of his offerings" (Heb. 11:4).

So the account of the contrast between Cain's and Abel's offerings is a foregleam of the teachings of the Old Testament prophets who consistently emphasized inward motivation as over against outward performance and ritual (see Amos 5:21-24; Hos. 6:6; Isa. 1:11-17; Mic. 6:6-8; Jer. 7:19,20). Samuel's words to Saul come immediately to mind: "Does the LORD delight in burnt offerings and sacrifices as much as in obeying the voice of the LORD? To obey is better than sacrifice, and to heed is better than the fat of rams" (1 Sam. 15:22). It is as true today as it was in Samuel's time that "man looks at the outward appearance, but the LORD looks at the heart" (16:7).

No wonder, then, that God "did not look with favor" on Cain and his offering! Cain, of course, could have taken the divine hint by expressing a heartfelt desire to humbly obey God from that time onward. But instead he "was very angry, and his face was downcast" (Gen. 4:5).

God's gracious and loving response to Cain's anger is coupled with a stern warning, making it clear that the choice is Cain's to make. If Cain does what is right the next time, says the Lord, he will be accepted and blessed. If he refuses to do so, however, sin is close at hand, waiting to gain the mastery over him.

The image of sin crouching at the door (see 4:7) is a vivid one indeed. In the original Hebrew text the phrase in question would be translated literally as follows: "At the door, sin is a croucher." In Akkadian (the language of ancient Assyria and Babylonia) the very same word translated here as *croucher* often refers to an evil demon who is depicted as lurking at the entrance of a building to threaten the people who are inside.[1] What a picture of sin! Waiting to pounce on its unsuspecting victims, sin is like an evil demon "crouching at your door; it desires to have you" (4:7)! Only the grace of a loving God, available to Cain for the asking, could save him from so fearful a menace.

But Cain would have none of that. He turned his back on God and slid deeper and deeper into sin.

Murder—and More (Gen. 4:8-16)

Cain's selfish attitude when he brought his offering to the Lord turned into anger when he realized that God did not look with favor on him. His anger was then replaced by jealousy toward his brother Abel. After deciding to get rid of Abel once and for all, Cain invited his brother to accompany him on a pleasant walk in the fields—out where God could not see him, Cain thought—and there he attacked Abel and killed him (see 4:8).

Cain's murder of Abel was all the more monstrous not only because it was the first one recorded in history but also because it was committed by a man against his brother—a fact the Bible emphasizes over and over (see Gen. 4:8,9,10,11; 1 John 3:12). It was also premeditated, since Cain carefully chose the time and place. And it was committed against an innocent man, a "righteous" man, as Jesus reminds us (see Matt. 23:35; see also Heb. 11:4; 1 John 3:12). Jesus even calls Abel a "prophet" (Luke 11:50,51), perhaps in the sense that Abel is still God's spokesman "even though he is dead" (Heb. 11:4).

Just as Paul expresses his fear that we could be deceived by Satan as Eve was (see 2 Cor. 11:3), so also John warns us not to follow Cain's example: "Do not be like Cain, who belonged to the evil one and murdered his brother . . . because his own actions were evil and his brother's were righteous" (1 John 3:12).

To try to cover up his brother's murder, Cain lied to

God. When asked where Abel was he said, "I don't know" (Gen. 4:9)—a deliberate and blatant falsehood. And then he continued to speak in a spirit of indifference and lack of concern: "Am I my brother's keeper?"

Those words have provided a rationale down through the centuries for people who have refused to get involved with the problems and difficulties that their neighbors are having. Like the priest and the Levite in the parable of the good Samaritan, whenever they see human misery and suffering they pass by "on the other side" (Luke 10:31,32). They have little or no sense of responsibility toward others. They are totally unlike the apostle Paul who said concerning his own ministry, "I am obligated both to Greeks and non-Greeks, both to the wise and the foolish" (Rom. 1:14). Far from wanting to destroy life as Cain did, Paul declared, "I have become all things to all men so that by all possible means I might save some" (1 Cor. 9:22).

On Mount Zion in modern Jerusalem stands a museum that contains the remains of a few of the six million Jews who were put to death by the Nazis during World War II. Included among the shocking exhibits are lampshades made of human skin and soap made of human fat. The museum itself is called the Chamber of Destruction, and the relics it contains are disquieting reminders of man's inhumanity to man. Outside the building is a simple plaque inscribed with a brief quotation from Genesis 4:10: "Listen! Your brother's blood cries out. . . ."

Cain had nothing to gain by lying to God, because his brother's blood gave him away. One of Adam's illustrious descendants, Judah, might have been thinking of the story of Cain and Abel when he said to his own brothers who had plotted to kill their brother

Joseph: "What will we gain if we kill our brother and cover up his blood? Come, let's . . . not lay our hands on him; after all, he is our brother, our own flesh and blood" (Gen. 37:26,27).

The blood of Abel—from time immemorial—is a most fitting symbol of the death of the innocent and righteous sufferer. But though Abel was righteous in a relative sense, he too was a sinner in need of God's grace and mercy, and therefore his shed blood carries no redemptive significance. As such it forms a powerful contrast to the blood of another righteous sufferer, to "the precious blood of Christ, a lamb without blemish or defect" (1 Pet. 1:19). In the final analysis it is Jesus' "sprinkled blood that speaks a better word than the blood of Abel" (Heb. 12:24).

Cain had disobeyed God, and disobedience always brings divine judgment (see Deut. 28:15). The ground had been cursed by God at the time of Adam's fall but hard work and painful toil would nevertheless make it possible for man to grow food for himself and his family (see Gen. 3:17-19). Now, however, Cain himself would be under a curse and would be driven from the very ground that he had soaked with his brother's blood (see 4:11). Before, Cain had worked the soil and it had produced food enough and to spare (see 4:2,3). But now, though he might labor long and hard, the ground would no longer yield its crops for him (see 4:12). The irony is obvious: The ground that had received the blood of Cain's dead brother would never again provide Cain with the livelihood he had always enjoyed. Far from being the settled farmer he had always been, he would become "a restless wanderer on the earth" (4:12,14).

For Cain, disobedience brought restlessness and

wandering. Other descendants of Adam would experience the same fate, and the "wandering Jew" would become a common motif in the history of the human race. The united witness of the people of Israel as they reflected on their turbulent past could be summed up in a single sentence: "My father was a wandering Aramean" (Deut. 26:5). If judgment on fields and flocks would begin the long list of God's curses for His people's disobedience (28:15-24), banishment and wandering and lack of repose would end that same list (see 28:64-68).

One would have thought that by this time Cain might have begun to feel a slight twinge of remorse, murderer that he was. But, incredible as it seems, he still did not ask God to forgive him for the death of Abel. His response to divine judgment was totally self-seeking: "My punishment is more than I can bear" (Gen. 4:13). He was being driven out from God's presence and protection, and he was afraid that whoever found him would kill him (see 4:14).

A question that is often asked about Genesis 4:17 is this: "Where did Cain get his wife?" A similar question can be asked of 4:14: "Who were the people that Cain was so afraid of?" The answer that is frequently given to the first question is that Cain married his own sister. That is entirely possible, of course, since when mankind first appeared on earth it would have been necessary for close relatives—even brothers and sisters—to intermarry.

But we cannot dispose of the second question quite so easily. The context (see Gen. 4:13-17), which speaks, for example, of "the land of Nod" and of "building a city," seems to presuppose considerable numbers of people. It would place a severe strain on the passage to insist that all of them were additional children of Adam and Eve. The very fact that Cain had to keep on the move appears to mean that he was afraid of far more people than the members of his immediate family.

A possible solution to this difficulty has already been suggested in chapter 4. If the theory of pre-Adamic hominids—who we know made razor-sharp weapons with which they killed animals—is correct, perhaps they are the enemies that Cain feared so much. Having much more intelligence than they, Cain and his family may have ultimately subdued them. But all such speculation takes us far beyond the evidence at our disposal.

In any event, the Lord graciously promised Cain that he would not be killed and put a mark on him "so that no one who found him would kill him" (4:15). The mark was perhaps a tattoo of some sort, and the Lord may have placed it on Cain's forehead (see Ezek. 9:4 for a possible parallel). But although we cannot be sure of the details, we can marvel that the Lord would promise to protect so violent a man as Cain.

This section of the narrative ends as Cain settles down east of Eden in a land called Nod. The name of his new home would continually remind him of the curse that had been placed on his life, since Nod in Hebrew means *wandering*.

How sad and sorry a tale this is! Cain's failure to give God his heart along with his offering made it impossible for God to look on him with favor. Cain then became angry at God and jealous of his brother. Jealousy, as it grew and festered, gave way to murder, and Cain was then forced to lie in order to cover it up. When his lie was found out and God announced judgment, Cain responded not with remorse over what he had done but with complaints about overly-severe punishment and with selfish concern about his personal well-being. Alienation from God was the final, awful result: "Cain went out from the LORD's presence" (Gen. 4:16).

Note

1. E.A. Speiser, *Genesis* (Garden City, NY: Doubleday & Company, Inc., 1964), p. 33.

7

TWO GENEALOGIES

Genesis 4:17—5:32

When God created man as male and female He said to them, "Be fruitful and increase in number; fill the earth and subdue it" (Gen. 1:27,28). As the crown and climax of God's creative activity, man was not intended to play a minor role in the ongoing purposes of God in the world. On the contrary, the divine plan thrust the human race onto center stage in the drama of history. God gave them a mandate of fruitfulness and increase and dominion, and it is to that mandate that the author of Genesis now turns.

He does so by giving two illustrations of how the descendants of Adam and Eve branched off into various family trees. The first illustration is a genealogy that serves to demonstrate how the cancer of sin was transmitted through Cain to the generations that followed him. The second is a genealogy that summarizes the time gap between the creation of man and the Flood.

The Genealogy of Pride (Gen. 4:17-24)

This section begins just as the previous section, 4:1-

16, did. The language is the same—only the characters are different: "Cain lay with [literally, knew] his wife, and she became pregnant and gave birth" (4:17). As God had promised, the human race would continue to propagate itself.

Although archaeologists have uncovered human settlements that go back to the earliest stages of civilization, the remains of ancient Jericho include the oldest ruins of a city found so far. An eminent British archaeologist, the late Kathleen Kenyon, excavated Jericho less than 30 years ago and found the fortified walls (including a massive defensive tower) of a Neolithic (New Stone Age) city at the lowest level of the site. Conservative dating for the building of that city places it at about 7000 B.C.

Cain doubtless lived before that time, and he built a city called Enoch (after the name of his son). Either its remains have been entirely obliterated or archaeologists have not yet found it. Of course it is possible that our dating methods are faulty and that archaeologists have indeed found Cain's city but have failed to recognize it as such. In any case, the existence of a city in Cain's time implies the presence of substantial numbers of people (see chapters 4 and 6 for a possible explanation of who those people were).

Adam's line through Cain contained exactly seven generations (Adam, Cain, Enoch, Irad, Mehujael, Methushael, Lamech). This fact serves as a subtle reminder of the importance of the number seven in these early chapters of Genesis (see chapter 3). *Seven* signifies *completion* in such cases, as in the Lord's statement that anyone who killed Cain would "suffer vengeance seven times over" (4:15).

Each of the seven names in the genealogy of Adam

through Cain is matched by a similar or identical name in Adam's line through Seth (though not in the same order) in Genesis 5:

Adam	Adam (5:1)
Cain	Kenan (5:12)
Enoch	Enoch (5:21)
Irad	Jared (5:18)
Mehujael	Mahalalel (5:15)
Methushael	Methuselah (5:25)
Lamech	Lamech (5:28)

The similarity between the two sets of names, which is even closer in the original Hebrew text, is probably to be accounted for by the selective nature of each genealogy. Both of them highlight the names of prominent family members and doubtless include gaps (as we shall see later).

Lamech, the seventh man in this genealogy, "married two women, one named Adah and the other Zillah" (4:19). Tempting though it might be to ascribe an element of perfection to such an arrangement (from A to Z), in the Hebrew alphabet *Adah* does not begin with the first letter and *Zillah* does not begin with the last! While the Old Testament nowhere condemns polygamy in an explicit and unambiguous way, it everywhere illustrates the sorrow and suffering that come to the family of a man who has more than one wife. Genesis 2:24 clearly states that God's original ideal for marriage was that it was to be a holy ordinance in which two people (not more than two) of the opposite sex (not of the same sex) were to "be united" and "become one flesh." Lamech's action in marrying more than one woman, then, is a further example of man's willful disobedience of God's commands and of his continued downward slide into ever-multiplying forms of sin.

Adah and Zillah each gave birth to two children. The only daughter among the four was Naamah, about whom we have no further information. But the names and occupations of the other three children tell an interesting story in their own right.

Lamech's three sons all had very similar names—Jabal, Jubal and Tubal-Cain—that have as their basis a Hebrew root that is very action-oriented and means *to bring, to carry, to lead*. Jabal was the ancestor of the nomadic shepherd way of life, of those who "live in tents and raise livestock" (4:20). Jubal, representing the artistic side of man, was the forerunner of musicians who play string or wind instruments, "the harp and flute" (4:21). Tubal-Cain represents the world's toolmakers (the Hebrew word *Cain* means *metalsmith*) as he "forged all kinds of tools out of bronze and iron" (4:22).

The mention of bronze and iron so early in human history presents something of a minor problem. The oldest known bronze artifacts date to about 3500 B.C., and the use of iron appears later still—about 1800 B.C.—and then only among the Hittites for several centuries (until about 1200 B.C.). We would suggest three possible solutions to this problem: (1) Adam is to be dated to a relatively late period; (2) early copper- and iron-smelting methods were lost and then rediscovered much later; (3) there are one or more time gaps in the line of Cain as recorded here. In our judgment a combination of (2) and (3) provides the most likely answer to the question we have raised.

The account of Cain's line concludes with a brief poem sometimes called "The Song of the Sword." Though its form may be beautiful, its content is barbaric. In retaliation for a wound he has received, Lamech decides to kill the young man who inflicted the wound. While God had promised to avenge Cain's death seven times (see 4:15), Lamech threatens vengeance 77 times over even for a wound (see 4:23,24).

So ends the "genealogy of pride"—pride that led to disobedience in marrying more than one wife, pride that carried with it the ever-present danger of self-glorification in the building of cities and the development of the arts and crafts, pride that spawned violence and the wanton destruction of human life. If humility is one of the most basic of all virtues, pride is one of the deadliest of all sins.

The Genealogy of Death (Gen. 4:25—5:32)

All is not lost, however. There is a second "written account of Adam's line" (5:1), this one tracing his descendants through a son named Seth. In contrast to the line of Cain, which was characterized by pride and self-indulgence, it is specifically said in connection with Seth's line that "at that time men began to call on the name of the LORD" (4:26). In contrast to the description of Cain's descendant Lamech as a sinful man, two of the men in Seth's genealogy—Enoch and Noah—are said to have "walked with God" (5:22,24; 6:9). For these reasons the two genealogies are sometimes called "the sinful line" and "the godly line" respectively.

The story of Adam's line through Seth is introduced in much the same way as Cain's genealogy was: "Adam lay with [literally, knew] his wife" (4:25; see 4:17). Eve gave birth to a son whom she named Seth, a word that sounds very much like the Hebrew verb translated *granted* in the statement giving the rationale behind the name: "God has granted me another child in place of Abel, since Cain killed him" (4:25). And so the text reminds us that Cain's line was the line of a murderer, while the genealogy of Seth holds out the promise of something far better. During the days of Seth's son Enosh people began to call on the name of the Lord, and that practice would often be followed by the best of Seth's descendants in the future (see Gen. 12:8; 26:25).

The opening verses of Genesis 5 take us back to the creation of man himself by using the language of 1:26-28. Just as God created man in His own image and likeness, so also Adam became the father of a son "in his own likeness, in his own image" (5:3). Such proverbs as "like begets like" and "like father, like son" gain a great measure of their power from biblical texts like these.

Unlike the seven-name line of Cain, the genealogy of Seth contains exactly 10 names from Adam through Noah. In this respect, and structurally as well, it is very similar to the genealogy in Genesis 11:10-26, which also contains exactly 10 names (this time from Noah's son Shem through Abram).

Each of the main paragraphs of the Genesis 5 genealogy follows the same basic pattern: "When So-and-So had lived x number of years, he became the father of Such-and-Such. And after he became the father of Such-and-Such, So-and-So lived y number of years and had other sons and daughters. Altogether, So-and-So lived z number of years, and then he died."

The doleful refrain, "and then he died," repeated over and over again throughout the chapter, has prompted us to entitle this section "the genealogy of death." Even virtuous men, however long their lives, must eventually die. God's judgment on Adam because of his sin extended universally to all mankind.

Well, not *quite* all mankind. In this very chapter we

note the fact that Enoch's paragraph does not end with the phrase "and then he died." It ends, rather, by telling us that "then he was no more, because God took him away" (5:24). He was translated from this life to the next without passing through the portals of death. As Hebrews 11:5 puts it: "By faith Enoch was taken from this life, so that he did not experience death; he could not be found, because God had taken him away. For before he was taken, he was commended as one who pleased God."

The verb *to take (away)* is used in a special sense in these verses. On rare occasions God *takes* one of His choice servants to Himself with an immediacy that eliminates the experience of death. The only other clear example in the Old Testament is that of Elijah, who was "taken" (2 Kings 2:10) directly to heaven "in a whirlwind" (2:11). But it may very well be that two of the psalms express the same confident hope (see Pss. 49:15; 73:24).

So although everyone else in Genesis 5 *died* (including Noah; see 9:29), Enoch "was no more, because God took him." Similarly, although everyone else in Genesis 5 *lived* (see for example 5:26), Enoch "walked with God" (5:22,24). The author is telling us that there is a vast difference between merely living on the one hand and walking with God on the other. Adam and Eve could have walked with God in the garden and so lived, but they chose rather to disobey God and so they died. To walk with God is to be righteous and blameless (see 6:9; 17:1); to walk with God is to please Him (see Heb. 11:5).

Enoch is the shining exception to the otherwise unrelieved gloom of Genesis 5. And what a contrast he presents to his numerical counterpart in Cain's line! Lamech, the seventh in the genealogy of Cain, is the very epitome of evil. But "Enoch, the seventh from Adam" (Jude 14) in the genealogy of Seth, "was commended as one who pleased God" (Heb. 11:5). The very length of his life was perfection itself: "365 years" (Gen. 5:23), 365 being the number of days in a full year. As Robert Ripley observed in a "Believe It or Not" column many years ago, although Methuselah was the oldest man in the Bible he was out-lived by his father Enoch, since Enoch never died!

Longevity and the Pre-Flood Patriarchs

As it turns out, Enoch's 365 years is the shortest life span in Genesis 5. Everyone else named in the chapter lived at least twice as long. In fact everyone except Lamech (see 5:31) lived to be about 900 years old (including Noah; see 9:29). How are we to understand these extraordinarily long life spans? Are the numbers to be taken literally, or did the author of Genesis have something else in mind in recording them for us?

Bible scholars today interpret these large numbers in many different ways. Some take them at face value claiming either that (1) climatic conditions before the Flood were ideal and were conducive to long life, or that (2) the pace of human life and the rate of human metabolism were much slower in those days, enabling people to live much longer, or that (3) the ravaging effects of sin on human longevity had not yet developed to their full extent before the Flood, or that (4) God in His sovereignty determined that certain special people should live unusually long lives and made it possible for them to do so. Others suggest that the solution to the problem lies in a combination of two or more of these proposals.

The main difficulty with these suggestions, however, is that paleoanthropologists have so far not uncovered any ancient skeletal remains that even remotely approach such advanced ages. If anything, scientific investigation has taught us that people had briefer life spans in the earliest periods of time than they do today. (This is not to deny, of course, that God could have supernaturally extended life in special cases if He had chosen to do so.)

Other scholars understand the numbers symbolically or take them to be literary devices or figures of speech. They observe, for example, the striking similarity between 4:24 which says that "if Cain is avenged seven times, then Lamech seventy-seven times," and 5:31 which tells us that the Cainite Lamech's namesake "lived 777 years." It is hard to read those numbers in other than a symbolic way, given the frequency of the number seven in the early chapters of Genesis.

Similarly, it has been noted that every number in Genesis 5 is either a multiple of five or a multiple of five to which seven has then been added. Seven is the number of perfection (as we have seen) and not necessarily in a strictly quantitative sense. In the case of Methuselah whose number is the largest in the chapter, the age is a multiple of five to which fourteen (twice seven) has then been added.[1] This means—so the theory goes—that Methuselah's age is doubly perfect and therefore will never be exceeded in any way.

Several other ancient genealogies from sources outside the Old Testament resemble Genesis 5 in a number of significant ways. Known as the Sumerian king lists, they seem to summarize the lengths of reign of various important kings of Sumer prior to the Flood. Two of them in particular—the Weld-Blundell 62 text and a Greek variant preserved by Berossus—form close parallels to Genesis 5 in three ways.

First, like Genesis 5 these two lists include exactly 10 names. When we remember that the Genesis 11 genealogy also has 10 names and that Genesis itself exhibits a literary structure that contains exactly 10 sections (see chapter 1 for details), we are perhaps justified in concluding that the most ancient accounts of man's origins favored the number 10 as a convenient literary device, especially in genealogical narratives.

Second, as in Genesis 5 the last name in the two Sumerian lists is that of the man who survived the flood (as we know from the Mesopotamian flood stories). Weld-Blundell 62 calls him *Ziusudra* (the Greek equivalent in the Berossus text is *Xisouthros*). In the Gilgamesh epic, the Babylonian parallel to the biblical flood narrative, he is known as *Utnapishtim*. Ziusudra and Utnapishtim find their historical counterpart in the biblical Noah.

Third, Genesis 5 exhibits unusually long life spans and the two Sumerian lists display incredibly long reigns for their kings. The very names of Ziusudra and Utnapishtim translate roughly as *Life of Distant Days,* reflecting the idea that long ages ago important people used to live and reign for periods of time that were exponentially greater than those we now experience. Three of the men in the Berossus list are said to have reigned for 64,800 years apiece, while three in Weld-Blundell 62 are stated to have been on the throne for a staggering 72,000 years! Such figures reduce even Methuselah to a babe in arms by comparison. By exaggerating figures beyond all reasonable belief, the Sumerian texts make it possible for us to characterize the Genesis 5 account as a model of restraint.

Genesis 5 and the Age of the Human Race

If the 10 numbers in Weld-Blundell 62 are added end

to end, the Sumerian kings in that list may have reigned
for 456,000 years in all. The figures is Genesis 5, however understood, total only a fraction of that amount. But the
Sumerian lists, since they claim to report the lengths of
reign of important kings, may provide us with an additional clue or two for a proper understanding of Genesis 5.

Most conservative scholars today have given up the
traditional assumption that Genesis 5 represents an exact
chronology, and the Sumerian king lists have added support to this newer understanding. The frequent occurrence
of 10 names in ancient family or regnal lines suggests
selectivity rather than the inclusion of every generation.
Only the most important names were included, and the
omission of unimportant names from ancient genealogies
was the rule rather than the exception.[2] To take a classic
example, Matthew 1:8 states that Joram was "the father of
Uzziah" (also known as Azariah). But 1 Chronicles
3:10,11 shows clearly that Joram was in fact the great-
great-grandfather of Uzziah.

This in turn demonstrates that the words *father, son,
beget,* and the like are much more flexible in the Bible
than we might at first imagine. For example Zilpah,
Leah's maidservant, is said to have given birth to her
great-grandchildren (Gen. 46:17,18). All of this implies
that there might very well be time gaps of substantial size
in Genesis 5.

Furthermore, the names in Genesis 5 might represent
families or dynasties rather than individuals. Just as *Israel*
or *David* in the Old Testament can be the name of a family
or tribe or dynasty as well as the name of an individual,
depending on the context, so also any of the names in
Genesis 5 could be understood in a sense other than that of
an individual person. Maybe all that Genesis 5 intends,

then, is to give us the names of important pre-flood dynasties together with the lengths of reign of their rulers. Needless to say, such an interpretation would have implications for a proper understanding of the life spans of ancient men and women and would lend more credence to the dating methods of paleoanthropologists.

In addition, the fact that Genesis 5 and 11 display a beautiful symmetry that suggests careful and intentional arrangement would seem to show that no continuous chronology is presupposed by them and that we should not try to calculate the date of Adam's creation from them (except in the most general way; see chapter 4 for details).

Finally, the Old Testament gives cumulative totals of years for such historic periods as "the length of time the Israelite people lived in Egypt" (430 years; Exod. 12:40) or the time span between the Exodus and the laying of the foundations of Solomon's Temple (480 years; 1 Kings 6:1). But no such totals are given for the time between Creation and the Flood or between Noah and Abraham.[3]

Taking such data into consideration, one recent evangelical student of Genesis comes to this conclusion: "Prior to the time of Abraham, there is no possible way to date the history of what we find in Scripture. . . . When the Bible itself reaches back and picks up events and genealogies in the time before Abraham, it never uses these early genealogies as a chronology. It never adds up these numbers for dating."[4]

But although the figures in Genesis 5 give us no chronological information, they are marvelously consistent within themselves. None of the men in Genesis 5, apart from Noah and his three sons (see 5:32), survived the Flood. In fact Methuselah (whether the name of a man or a dynasty) died in the very year of the Flood itself: The figures in 5:25, 5:28 and 7:6 add up to precisely 969!

The birth of Noah, whose name sounds like the Hebrew word for *comfort* (see 5:29), is ominous in its import as well. The Lord had cursed the ground because of man's sin soon after Creation (see 3:17). Genesis 5:29 echoes that curse and prepares us for a second divine judgment of the earth that would prove to be even more devastating than the first.

Notes

1. U. Cassuto, *A Commentary on the Book of Genesis, Part I: From Adam to Noah* (Jerusalem: Magnes Press, 1961), pp. 259,260.
2. On this whole section see especially W.H. Green, "Primeval Chronology," in W.C. Kaiser, ed., *Classical Evangelical Essays in Old Testament Interpretation* (Grand Rapids: Baker Book House, 1972), pp. 13-28.
3. O.T. Allis, *God Spake by Moses* (Nutley, NJ: The Presbyterian and Reformed Publishing Company, 1951), p. 22.
4. F.A. Schaeffer, *Genesis in Space and Time* (Downers Grove, IL: Inter-Varsity Press, 1972), p. 124.

8

THE EXTENT OF SIN BEFORE THE FLOOD

Genesis 6:1-8

Was Lamech, in his polygamy and selfishnness and pride and violence (see Gen. 4:19-24), the wickedest man who ever lived? We cannot say for sure, of course—but he would obviously be a prime candidate for that unenviable designation. In any case, sin in its worst forms reached epidemic proportions in the days before the Flood. And although the godly walk of Enoch (see 5:21-24), the expectant spirit of the second Lamech (see 5:28,29) and the blameless life of Noah (see 6:8,9) might delay the divine judgment for a time, it could not postpone it indefinitely.

Sons of God and Daughters of Men (Gen. 6:1-3)

As the population of the earth continued to increase, more and more marriages would take place. It is in this connection that we are told that the "sons of God" married the "daughters of men."

Who were these pre-Flood sons of God? Two main interpretations have been held down through the centuries.

First, the phrase "sons of God" frequently refers to angels in the Bible. A good example is Job 1:6; 2:1 where we read that "the angels [literally, sons of God] came to present themselves before the LORD." Satan was among them, and since Satan is a fallen angel there can be no reasonable doubt about the meaning of *sons of God* in this passage.

Although Psalm 29:1 is not quite so clear an example, most commentators feel that angels are in view in that passage as well: "Ascribe to the LORD, O mighty ones [literally, sons of God], ascribe to the LORD glory and strength." When read in the light of its context, the verse seems to be encouraging the angels to praise and worship God in the spirit of Isaiah 6:1-3.

Sons of God in such passages is not to be understood literally, of course. Although other ancient religions had highly developed cosmogonies (mythological stories about gods who had wives, children and other relatives), the religion of the Old Testament teaches that there is only one God, who has neither family nor rivals. In fact, the Hebrew language did not even have a word for *goddess*. When it wanted to refer to a female pagan deity it had to use its word for *god* as in 1 Kings 11:33 where the text mentions "Ashtoreth the goddess [literally, god] of the Sidonians."

When *sons of God* means *angels*, then, it uses the word *son* not in the sense of physical offspring but in the sense of a member of a group. Just as *sons of the prophets* means *members of a prophetic guild*, so also *sons of God* can mean *members of the divine council* or the like. God is sometimes pictured figuratively as having celestial advisors in His court, advisors with whom He sometimes talks and shares information as in Genesis 3:22: "The man has now become like one of us, knowing good and evil."[1]

Another point in favor of interpreting sons of God as angels in Genesis 6 is the New Testament teaching concerning fallen angels. First Peter 3:19,20, which talks about "the spirits in prison who disobeyed long ago when God waited patiently in the days of Noah while the ark was being built," is often thought to refer to such angels. The passage, however, is difficult at best and does not lend itself to confident conclusions.

Second Peter 2:4 would seem to be more to the point: "God did not spare angels when they sinned, but sent them to hell, putting them into gloomy dungeons to be held for judgment." But the main problem with this verse is that it appears to refer to a rebellion against God that took place before the fall of man in Genesis 3—indeed, a rebellion that was severely judged by God. Nothing is said about judging angels in Genesis 6:1-3, so we would be overstepping our bounds if we insisted that 2 Peter 2:4 and Genesis 6 referred to the same event.

A third New Testament passage that some claim is related to Genesis 6 is Jude 6: "The angels who did not keep their positions of authority but abandoned their own home—these he has kept in darkness, bound with everlasting chains for judgment on the great Day." But this verse is much more similar to 2 Peter 2:4 than it is to Genesis 6:1-3. Its references to judgment and darkness are out of keeping with the context at the beginning of Genesis 6.

To summarize, then, Genesis 6:1-3 bears only a superficial resemblance to the New Testament texts described here. It is not at all clear that the Genesis passage portrays fallen angels or disobedient spirits. If the "sons of God" in 6:2 and 4 are indeed angels, that identification will have to be confirmed on other grounds.

And it is at this point that the identification begins to break down. Since this would be the first mention of angels in Scripture, why would the author not simply call them angels in order to avoid all ambiguity? While it is true that ancient mythologies often include stories about gods cohabiting with women, the Genesis account is not mythical in form or intention and is set forth as sober history.

But the decisive blow against the angel interpretation is Jesus' response to the Sadducees is Luke 20:34-36: "The people of this age marry and are given in marriage. But those who are considered worthy of taking part in that age and in the resurrection from the dead will neither marry nor be given in marriage, and they can no longer die; for they are like the angels." Jesus tells us here that angels do not marry, and His statement would flatly contradict Genesis 6:2 and 4 if the "sons of God" in that passage are angels.

Second, "sons of God" refers to men. In the Old Testament, however, the phrase *sons of God* is never used unambiguously to refer to human beings. But equivalent expressions are fairly common. A few examples will suffice.

In Deuteronomy 14:1 Moses says to the people of Israel, "You are the children [literally, sons] of the LORD your God." Because of their sin it is said of them that they are "no longer his children [literally, sons]" (32:5). Else-

where the psalmist says to God that under certain circumstances he "would have betrayed this generation of
your children [literally, sons]" (Ps. 73:15). Isaiah 43:6
quotes God as saying, "Bring my sons from afar." And in
Hosea 1:10 the people of Israel are called "sons of the
living God."

The New Testament evidence is, if anything, even
stronger. Adam is called "the son of God" in Luke 3:38.
Christians are referred to as "children of God" in 1 John
3:1,2,10. But the most impressive passage is the section
from Luke 20 that we quoted earlier. There we read that
people who are considered worthy of taking part "in the
resurrection from the dead will neither marry nor be given
in marriage, and they can no longer die; for they are like
the angels. They are God's children [literally, sons of
God]." The text itself tells us that people, though not
angels, are nevertheless sons of God.

From the standpoint of biblical usage, then, there can
be no objection to interpreting "sons of God" in Genesis 6
as men. In fact, such an understanding is much to be
preferred in the context of the passage. A brief paragraph
about angels would be a very abrupt interruption in the
flow of the story. But if the sons of God are men, who are
the "daughters of men" (6:2,4)?

Sons of God in this passage means, more specifically,
godly men. Since they chose to marry daughters of men
rather than daughters of God (that is, godly women—see,
for example, Isa. 43:6—a live possibility for them, it
would seem), that choice proved to be unwise. The sons
of God are no doubt the descendants of Seth, whose line is
summarized in Genesis 5. They chose either to marry
sinful women within their own lineage or to intermarry
with members of the wicked line of Cain. Although our

personal preference is the latter, the results were disastrous in either case, as we shall see. Genesis 6:1,2 describes the intermarriage of the Sethites of Genesis 5 with the Cainites of Genesis 4.

The Lord's response to this unhappy state of affairs is likewise subject to more than one interpretation, since the key verb in 6:3 can be translated in at least two ways: (1) "My Spirit will not *remain in* man forever," or (2) "My Spirit will not *contend with* man forever." If the former is correct, then the text is saying that man's life span will be limited to 120 years from this point on because God will not allow the breath of life to remain in him indefinitely. If the latter is correct, then the text states that 120 years will be the period of grace between the time of God's pronouncement and the arrival of divine judgment. The former is contradicted by the genealogy in Genesis 11:10-26, while the latter is substantiated by 1 Peter 3:20: "God waited patiently in the days of Noah while the ark was being built."

The teaching of Genesis 6:3 is solemn indeed. It reminds us that though God is merciful and patient, though He is compassionate and slow to become angry (see Exod. 34:6), the Holy Spirit's convicting influence can be stifled and quenched by our willful rejection and rebellion. Eventually, if we continue to harden our hearts against Him, He will stop speaking to us altogether. At that point—the point of no return—judgment becomes inevitable.

The Nephilim (Gen. 6:4)

According to Numbers 13:33 the Nephilim were the ancestors of Anak and his descendants, some of whom settled in the vicinity of Hebron (see Judg. 1:20). They were people of great size and strength (Num. 13:28-33) and earlier English versions translated *Nephilim* in Genesis 6:4 as "giants."

Although the word itself appears to be a proper noun and is therefore the name of a tribe or people, in Hebrew it means literally *fallen ones*. As such it fits the context admirably because it describes the moral and spiritual depravity of the human race just before the Flood. Though the Nephilim were "the heroes of old, men of renown," they were wicked sinners in the eyes of a holy God. The depths of evil into which they had fallen, starkly portrayed in the next few verses of Genesis, had made them ripe for judgment.

Sin at Its Worst (Gen. 6:5-8)

In the days before the Flood, sin had become pervasive and all-encompassing. Its evil tentacles reached into every nook and cranny of a person's life, and no one was ever free of its influence. The description of the awfulness of sin in Genesis 6:5 would be hard to match anywhere else in Scripture. Man's wickedness had become so great that "every inclination of the thoughts of his heart was only evil all the time." It is not merely that he harbored a somewhat sinful thought once in a while. On the contrary, his depravity was total: *Every* tendency of his *innermost* thoughts was *only* evil *all* the time.

Genesis 8:21 quotes a portion of 6:5 and observes that "all the time" means "from childhood" on. Original sin among human beings began with Adam and Eve, but each of us participates in original sin in another sense as we begin to exhibit sinful traits soon after we are born. David confessed that fact after he had committed adultery with Bathsheba: "I have been a sinner from birth, sinful from the time my mother conceived me" (Ps. 51:5; see also 58:3).

"The LORD saw how great man's wickedness on the earth had become" in the days before the Flood (Gen. 6:5), and He witnesses our evil actions and motivations today as well. At this very moment He "looks down from heaven on the sons of men to see if there are any who understand, any who seek God" (Ps. 14:2). But His verdict is the same as it was in the days of Noah: "All have turned aside, they have together become corrupt; there is no one who does good, not even one" (14:3). The cancer of sin rages through us and strikes at the very core of our being. "The heart is deceitful above all things and beyond cure" (Jer. 17:9).

Before the Flood man's "heart was only evil," and therefore God's "heart was filled with pain" (Gen. 6:5,6). Man's sin is always God's sorrow. The Lord was "grieved" that He had made man in the first place. Our God is a loving heavenly Father, and His heart breaks when we disobey Him. To cause Him such grief is the height of ingratitude in the light of all that He has done for us in Christ. That is why Paul says to us, "Do not grieve the Holy Spirit of God" (Eph. 4:30).

As we stated earlier in this chapter, mankind before the Flood had sunk to such depths of moral and spiritual degradation that God had no alternative but to punish them. Having passed the point of no return, they were ripe for divine judgment. When God is grieved by man's sin, His heart is filled with pain because He loves us. But the grief that man's sin brings to God's heart also has its darker side—in cases like the one described here, it issues in divine judgment. Though God loves the sinner, He judges his sin.

Scripture teaches that God responds negatively to sin but positively to repentance. When we forsake our sin and turn to Him in repentance, He forsakes His intention to judge us and turns to us in love. The reverse is also true, however, as Jeremiah so clearly outlines both alternatives: "Then the word of the LORD came to me: . . . 'If at any time I announce that a nation or kingdom is to be uprooted, torn down and destroyed, and if that nation I warned repents of its evil, then I will relent and not inflict on it the disaster I had planned. And if at another time I announce that a nation or kingdom is to be built up and planted, and if it does evil in my sight and does not obey me, then I will reconsider the good I had intended to do for it' " (Jer. 18:5,7-10).

God's judgment of pre-Flood mankind was not inevitable—at least not at first. As long as His Spirit contended with them (see Gen. 6:3) they had the opportunity to repent. But when God's deadline for repentance had passed He announced that He would "wipe mankind . . . from the face of the earth" (6:7). He doubtless did so reluctantly, since they were the crown of His creative activity. But they had defaced the divine image in which they had been made. It was beyond restoration, and God decided to destroy all mankind. Human sin had so tainted the entire created order that all the animals and birds would die as well. No life of any sort would remain.

"But Noah found favor in the eyes of the LORD" (6:8). Noah's life is the one point of light shining bravely through the awful darkness that is about to engulf the world. Though he was a "righteous man" (6:9), however, he and his family would survive the waters of the flood not because of his goodness but because of God's grace.

And so it is with us today. We who are Christians

would do well to remind ourselves often that the Lord has "saved us, not because of righteous things we had done, but because of his mercy" (Titus 3:5).

Note

1. G.L. Archer, *Decision* (May, 1979), p. 14.

9
PREPARING FOR THE FLOOD

Genesis 6:9—7:10

"This is the account of Noah" (Gen. 6:9) is the title of the third major section in the primeval history recorded in Genesis 1—11. By far the longest of the five sections that constitute that history, it tells the story of the flood that destroyed sinful mankind in the days of Noah. It describes the divine judgment on the human race that came because of their rebellion against God.

Needless to say, biblical events did not take place in a historical vacuum. The people of the Old Testament were very much a part of the times and places in which they lived. Genesis 1—36, for example, has Mesopotamia as the historical and cultural background of the people involved for the most part, while 37—50 finds them in the land of Egypt.

Although Genesis 1—2 bears only a superficial resemblance to various Mesopotamian creation stories, we have already noted several similarities between Genesis 5 and the Sumerian king lists (see chapter 7). Genesis 6—9, however, has parallels from Mesopotamia—both Sumerian and Babylonian—that are closer still.

Of all the Mesopotamian flood stories, the eleventh tablet of the Babylonian epic of Gilgamesh (named after its main character) bears the most striking resemblances to Genesis 6—9. It includes (1) a divine warning of the impending flood, (2) the building of a ship coated with pitch, (3) the gathering of representative animals and birds to save them from the flood, (4) the ship's coming to rest on a mountain, (5) the sending out of birds to reconnoiter, and (6) the offering of a sacrifice after leaving the ship.

Differences between the Babylonian and biblical stories, however, are equally impressive: (1) The Babylonian ship is in the shape of a cube, while Noah's ark has the general proportions of modern ships and is therefore much more seaworthy than its Babylonian counterpart; (2) the order of sending out the birds is different in the two accounts; (3) the Babylonian flood lasts 14 days while the biblical flood lasts more than a year; (4) the Babylonian flood has only two survivors (Utnapishtim and his wife), the biblical flood eight; (5) the two Babylonian survivors achieve immortality after the flood, while Noah and his family eventually die; and (6) the Babylonian account is grossly polytheistic (the gods "cower like dogs" next to a wall and "gather like flies" above a sacrifice),[1] while the Genesis account knows only the one true God.

Although the Gilgamesh epic is older than the present form of the Genesis story, both are probably dependent on a still earlier account. The superintending influence of the Holy Spirit preserved the sober historical character of the biblical flood story and kept it from being tainted by the polytheism that so debased the Babylonian narrative.

Righteousness in the Midst of Corruption (Gen. 6:9-12)

Noah's godly life is described in three complementary ways in Genesis 6:9. Like John the Baptist (see Mark 6:20) and Simeon (see Luke 2:25), Noah was a "righteous" man, satisfying the standards established for him by a holy God. Like Abraham (see Gen. 17:1) and Job (see Job 1:1), Noah was "blameless," giving his contemporaries no excuse to criticize his conduct. And like Enoch (see Gen. 5:22,24), Noah "walked with God," exhibiting in word and deed the closeness of his fellowship with the Lord.

Although Noah's three sons—Shem, Ham, and Japheth—had already been mentioned earlier in the account (see 5:32), their names and their relationship to their father appear again in the context of his righteous life (see 6:10). The reference to them here would seem to be superfluous unless we assume its purpose to be that Noah's sons shared his moral and spiritual ideals. That in turn would help to explain why Shem, Ham and Japheth, as a part of their father's godly family, were saved from the Flood along with Noah himself.

The rest of mankind, however, was very wicked indeed. Three times in 6:11,12 we are told how "corrupt" the earth had become. In Genesis 1 God saw how good, how "very good" (1:31), His entire creation was. In Genesis 6 God sees how thoroughly corrupt "all the people on earth" (6:12) have become as a result of the entrance of sin into the human heart. Because violence and evil reign everywhere, God has decided to destroy all mankind and to make Noah and his family the ancestors of a new humanity.

The Command to Build the Ark (Gen. 6:13-22)

An enormous ship was the vehicle that God chose to

use to save the righteous few. The Hebrew word translated as *ark* in the Flood story is used in the Old Testament almost exclusively to refer to Noah's ship. It appears elsewhere only in Exodus 2, where it is translated as *basket* (see Exod. 2:3,5). As the ark saved Noah and seven others from a watery grave, so the basket saved the baby Moses from a similar fate. And both the ark and the basket were coated with pitch (see Gen. 6:14; Exod. 2:3). If Moses was indeed the author of both Genesis and Exodus, these striking similarities between the story of his own deliverance and that of Noah must have impressed him deeply.

The wood that the ark was made of was probably cypress, although we cannot be sure. It had three decks, which in turn were divided into rooms. One interpretation of Genesis 6:16 pictures the ark as having a series of small windows running the entire length of the vessel 18 inches from the top. The windows would admit light and air, while an overhanging roof would keep the rain from coming in. The door in the side of the ark was its only entrance and exit.

The ark's dimensions were truly remarkable for its time. It was "450 feet long, 75 feet wide and 45 feet high" (6:15). Modern ocean liners rarely exceed twice the length of Noah's ark. To compare it with something perhaps more familiar to us, we observe that the ark was half again as long as a football field!

What did the ark look like? Only its dimensions are given to us, so we are free to speculate concerning its shape. It probably did not resemble modern ships because such construction requires the skills of expert shipwrights. Nor would a simple rectangular shape have been suitable since Noah then would have been forced to provide the vessel with a maze of supporting beams and braces, drastically reducing the living space available for himself, his family and all the animals. In any case a rectangular ark would not have been buoyant enough to carry its huge load and would not have floated evenly in the water without a massive keel.

Meir Ben-Uri, an Israeli scholar, has developed an attractive theory concerning the shape of the ark. He believes that it was a long flattened box, its two ends shaped like lozenges. A straight line joining any two of the acute angles in the cross section of a ship built in such a shape would be exactly parallel to the surface of the water when the ark was afloat. The obtuse-angled bottom of the ship would have served as a rudimentary keel as it provided stability and kept the ark from capsizing. Ben-Uri says that such a ship would have weighed about 6,000 tons and have had a carrying capacity of about 15,000 tons.[2] There would have been plenty of room for Noah's family, the animals, and enough food for all of them during the year they spent on board.

But whatever the shape of the ark, its declared purpose was to provide sanctuary for eight people and thousands of animals through the crisis of the Flood. The devastating power of the floodwaters would totally destroy all other life "under the heavens" (6:17; see 2 Pet. 3:6). Every creature that had "the breath of life" in it would die, but the Lord would "keep alive" Noah, his three sons, Noah's wife and his sons' wives (Gen. 6:19,20). The story of Noah's salvation from the Flood is used in the Bible to typify God's deliverance of all who trust in Him (see Heb. 11:7; 2 Pet. 2:5) and provides a beautiful symbol of baptism as well (see 1 Pet. 3:20,21).

The story also illustrates another important biblical

principle. While God bestows His saving grace and love on individuals, He is concerned about their families as well. Although numerous passages could be mentioned in this regard, we call attention here to only a few examples: Genesis 17:7-27; Deuteronomy 30:19; Psalm 78:1-7; 102:28; 103:17,18; 112:1,2; Acts 2:38,39; 1 Corinthians 7:14. In the New Testament the principle is well summarized in Acts 16:31: "Believe in the Lord Jesus, and you will be saved—you and your household."

God announced in advance that He would establish His covenant with Noah (see Gen. 6:18), a covenant that Noah would fully understand only after the Flood was over (see 9:8-17). It would include the promise that such a destructive flood would never again wipe out all mankind. But implicit in its provisions would also be the divine mandate to "be fruitful and increase in number," to "fill the earth and subdue it" (1:28; see 9:1,7). The same command that God gave when He created man would also be necessary if the earth was to be repopulated after the Flood.

Noah was also to lead into the finished ark a minimum of two of every "kind" (see chapter 2) of bird and animal in order to restock the earth after the floodwaters receded. That two is intended as a minimal figure is clear from 7:2,3: "Take with you seven of every kind of clean animal, a male and its mate, and two of every kind of unclean animal, a male and its mate, and also seven of every kind of bird, male and female, to keep their various kinds alive throughout the earth." Whether "seven" in these verses means literally seven or seven pairs or even several (see 1 Sam. 2:5; 2 Kings 4:35), it is clear that although only two of every kind of unclean animal may have been needed, many more than two of every kind of clean animal were required. This is because the unclean animals had only to reproduce themselves after the Flood, while the clean animals would not only have to reproduce themselves but would also be needed for the burnt offerings that Noah would sacrifice (see Gen. 8:20). Only animals that were ceremonially clean could properly be offered to God.

Apparently all the animals would "come to" Noah voluntarily (see 6:20). It would seem that he would not have to hunt them down or look for them in remote places. Their natural instinct for self-preservation, energized by a special act of God, would bring them unerringly to Noah's ark.

The story emphasizes Noah's obedience in fulfilling every order that God issued to him. We are told over and over that he "did everything just as God commanded him" (6:22; see also 7:5,9,16). Because he was righteous, he obeyed whenever God spoke and did whatever God told him to do, however strange or unusual the command may have seemed to him. In so doing he anticipated the quality of prompt obedience that would later characterize his descendant Abraham (see 12:4; 17:23; 21:14; 22:3).

The Command to Enter the Ark (Gen. 7:1-5)

For the second time in the story, Noah is said to be "righteous," again in contrast to nearly everyone else (7:1; see 6:9). And as his righteousness led him to obey God, so also God would single him and his family out for salvation because the Lord had found him righteous.

The number seven continues to figure prominently in the Genesis narrative. In addition to the seven (or seven pairs) of every kind of clean animal discussed above, seven was the number of days between the Lord's command to enter the ark and His sending of rain on the earth (see 7:4). Needless to say, the floodwaters came in seven days as a result of the rain just as God had said they would (see 7:10).

"Forty days and forty nights" would be the amount of time that the rain would continue to fall (see 7:4,12). That length of time, whether understood literally every time it occurs or figuratively in some cases, was often used as the temporal backdrop for critical periods in the history of God's people. Moses stayed on Mount Sinai 40 days and 40 nights (see Exod. 24:18), and there the Lord gave him the two stone tablets of the covenant on which the Ten Commandments were written (see Deut. 9:11). Jesus fasted 40 days and 40 nights in the desert (see Matt. 4:2), and there the devil tempted Him three times (see 4:3-11).

After the Lord told Noah that the rains were about to fall He repeated His earlier words of judgment: "I will wipe from the face of the earth every living creature I have made" (Gen. 7:4). Those are the last recorded words of God to Noah until after the Flood itself, more than a year later. God's final speech, before the Flood, begins with the words, "Go into the ark" (7:1); His first speech after the Flood begins with the words, "Come out of the ark" (8:16). The text of Genesis represents the year between those two speeches as a time when God is silent, a time of patient waiting for Noah and his family.

Entering the Ark (Gen. 7:6-10)

Noah reached the advanced age of 500 years before Shem, Ham and Japheth were born (see 5:32), and he was 600 years old "when the floodwaters came on the earth" (7:6). If the 120 years of 6:3 were the period of grace between the time of God's pronouncement in that verse and the arrival of divine judgment (as we argued in chapter 8), the period had to begin before Noah's five-hundredth year. At any rate, Noah's sons were able to assist him in building the ark only after the 120 years were already well underway. In fact it would seem that God's command to Noah to build the ark was not issued until after all three sons were born (see 6:10-13), reducing the amount of time traditionally allowed for its construction and making the feat itself all the more amazing.

Noah and his family entered the completed ark "to escape the waters of the flood" (7:7). What were other people doing just before the floodwaters came?

In a graphic description of His second coming, Jesus gives us a vivid portrayal of the situation in those early days: "As it was in the days of Noah, so it will be at the coming of the Son of Man. For in the days before the Flood, people were eating and drinking, marrying and giving in marriage, up to the day Noah entered the ark; and they knew nothing about what would happen until the flood came and took them all away" (Matt. 24:37-39). The tragedy of defying God over and over again, of toying with His patience continually and persistently, is that eventually the time of repentance passes by and it becomes too late to seek His forgiveness. When the Flood came, everyone outside Noah's immediate family was beyond hope and doomed to destruction.

And as it was then so it will be when Jesus returns: "The Lord is not slow in keeping his promise, as some understand slowness. He is patient with you, not wanting anyone to perish, but everyone to come to repentance. But the day of the Lord will come like a thief. The heavens will disappear with a roar; the elements will be destroyed by fire, and the earth and everything in it will be laid bare" (2 Pet. 3:9,10).

Seven days after Noah's family and the birds and animals entered the ark, the floodwaters inundated the earth.

Notes

1. See E.A. Speiser in *Ancient Near Eastern Texts Relating to the Old Testament,* J.B. Pritchard, ed. (Princeton: Princeton University Press, 1955), 2nd ed., pp. 94,95.
2. *The Jerusalem Post* (October 10, 1967).

10

THE FLOOD: JUDGMENT AND REDEMPTION

Genesis 7:11—8:19

The biblical flood story provides unforgettable illustrations of divine judgment and divine redemption. Judgment stands out in bold relief in the account of the relentless rising of the waters (see Gen. 7:11-24), a section that divides into two parts: the beginning of the Flood (see 7:11-16) and the continuing of the Flood (see 7:17-24). Redemption is stressed in the account of the gradual receding of the waters (see 8:1-19), a section that also divides into two parts: the cessation of the flood (see 8:1-14) and the exit from the ark (see 8:15-19).

Before looking at each of the four subsections in detail, it will be useful for us to examine the chronological framework in which the flood narrative itself is set. Since "Noah was six hundred years old when the floodwaters came on the earth" (7:6) his age will be the year-date in our series of shorthand notations as we list the critical events in their proper order. "2/17/600," for example, will be our way of writing "the six hundredth year of Noah's life, on the seventeenth day of the second month" (7:11).

2/17/600: The great Flood begins as water pours down from above and bursts forth from below (see 7:11).

For 40 days and 40 nights the rain continues to fall (see 7:4,12) and the waters continue to rise (see 7:17).

For a total of 150 days the waters flood the earth and the ark floats on them (see 7:24; 8:3).

7/17/600: The ark comes to rest on the mountains of Ararat at the end of exactly 150 days (see 8:4).

10/1/600: The tops of the mountains become visible as the waters gradually recede (see 8:5).

After 40 days Noah sends out a raven from the ark and the bird flies back and forth until it finds a dry nesting place (see 8:6,7).

Sometime later (probably seven days, since 8:10 mentions "seven more days") Noah sends out a dove that returns when it finds no dry place to land on (see 8:8,9).

After seven more days Noah sends the dove out again and it returns the same evening carrying a freshly plucked olive leaf (see 8:10,11).

After waiting another seven days Noah sends the dove out once more, and this time it does not return (see 8:12).

1/1/601: The floodwaters have now receded to the extent that the surface of the ground is dry (see 8:13).

2/27/601: The water has now dried up entirely, and the earth is completely dry (see 8:14).

Even though some of the sevens and tens and forties in this chronological sketch may be figurative or round numbers rather than precise numbers, the first and last dates clearly demonstrate that the great Flood lasted for over a year.

The Beginning of the Flood (Gen. 7:11-16)

Anyone who has ever experienced even a minor flood knows something of the devastating force generated by water that breaks free of whatever was holding it back. But we can only dimly imagine what it must have been like on the day when "all the springs of the great deep burst forth, and the floodgates of the heavens were opened" (7:11). The incredible power and speed of massive quantities of water gushing out of subterranean springs and pouring down from the skies above caught everyone by surprise—everyone, that is, but "Noah and his sons, Shem, Ham and Japheth, together with his wife and the wives of his three sons" (7:13). By entering the ark on the day the flood began, they and the animals they had gathered escaped with their lives.

The story of the onset of the great Flood is a masterpiece of brief but vivid description. Upheavals beneath the ocean floor are portrayed as the bursting forth of springs, and the falling of torrential rains is compared to the opening of floodgates. We are served notice right from the start that this was no ordinary flood.

The biblical flood account gave rise to the use of untamed and unleashed waters as a literary symbol of sudden and overwhelming judgment in the writings of Old Testament poets. The psalmist in his agony cries out to God: "Deep calls to deep in the roar of your waterfalls; all your waves and breakers have swept over me" (Ps. 42:7). A poet in the same tradition voices his complaint to the Lord: "Your wrath lies heavily upon me; you have overwhelmed me with all your waves" (Ps. 88:7). The ancient Israelites were reminded by their flood narrative that water can crush as well as cleanse.

Five main categories of animate life are mentioned in

the Genesis 1 creation account: sea creatures, birds, wild animals, livestock, and creatures that move along the ground (see Gen. 1:21-25). Pairs of all the members of each category went into the ark with Noah (see 7:14,15)—each category, that is, except one: the sea creatures. The flood was so widespread that only they could remain outside the ark and survive. After the floodwaters had receded completely, however, they would once again fall under human dominion together with all the other animals (see 9:2).

The paragraph that describes the beginning of the Flood concludes by telling us that the animals entered the ark "as God had commanded Noah. Then the LORD shut him in" (7:16). Why the sudden shift in the divine name in the space of such a few words?

We observed in chapter 3 that in the Old Testament "LORD" is the intimate, personal name of God and emphasizes His work as Redeemer, while "God" is His more formal and impersonal name and focuses on His work as Creator. The compound name "LORD God" that occurs so often in Genesis 2 shows us that both names are titles of one and the same God.

In 7:16, then, it is God as Creator who issues commands to Noah, but it is God in His other role as the redeeming Lord who gently closes the door of Noah's ark and shuts him in. The ark is the vehicle of salvation for Noah and his family. Much later, Jonah would state a very simple truth after being delivered from a watery grave himself: "Salvation comes from the LORD" (Jon. 2:9).

The Floodwaters Continue to Rise (Gen. 7:17-24)

The previous section was the only major paragraph in the flood story that used both of the most common Old

Testament names for God. The section now before us, by contrast, is the only major paragraph in the flood narrative that omits the name of God entirely. The reason is clear: As soon as Noah and his family are safely in the ark, God unleashes the full fury of His wrath on the rest of mankind. He turns his back on them, and the floodwaters are free to do their awful work of judgment. The people outside the ark had sinned once too often against God, and He left them to their own devices.

The language used in these verses is vigorous indeed and leaves no doubt as to its intention. We are told over and over that the waters increased and rose greatly, that they covered all the high mountains, that every living thing that moved on the earth "perished," "died," "was wiped out" (7:21,22,23). The flood was so massive that "only Noah was left, and those with him in the ark" (Gen. 7:23). At their greatest height, the floodwaters covered the highest mountains "to a depth of more than twenty feet" (7:20). Since the ark was "45 feet high" (6:15), the waters were deep enough to allow the ark to float freely and to keep it from scraping bottom.

When God first created man, He breathed "into his nostrils the breath of life" (2:7). But just as God, because of human sin, banished the first couple from the garden where the tree of life was located, so also now, because of human sin, God sends the great Flood in order that every living thing that has "the breath of life in its nostrils" will die (7:22). As the ground was cursed because of man's original sin (see 3:17), so also now the earth and all its creatures great and small are judged because of man's disobedience and rebellion against God (see 7:21-23). The fatal effects of the sin of man are experienced by all other living creatures as well.

It will be useful for us at this point to summarize a number of principles of divine judgment as illustrated by the Flood.

First, *God's judgments are not arbitrary*. Our God is not capricious in His decisions to judge His creatures. Divine judgment is always related to human wickedness. The Lord was determined to wipe mankind from the face of the earth because of their violent and corrupt behavior. Their conduct caused Him grief and filled His heart with pain and so He decided to put an end to all the people on earth (see 6:5-13).

Second, *God always announces His judgments beforehand*. Once having made a decision to judge His sinful creatures, God warns them of the impending judgment. He does not sneak up on them unawares and judge them without first telling them of His plans. Far from being a distant and hidden God who conceals His desires from His people, He proclaims to them in no uncertain terms and in a variety of ways (see Heb. 1:1,2) what He intends to do. In the case of the Flood the Lord revealed to Noah that He was going to destroy the earth and every living creature on it (see Gen. 6:13).

Although God sometimes announces coming judgment directly, He more often does so through His chosen servants. While the ark was being built Noah, "a preacher of righteousness" (2 Pet. 2:5), proclaimed a message of condemnation to the world of his day and in so doing witnessed to the vitality of his own faith (see Heb. 11:7). Himself warned, he also warned others.

Third, *God always grants time for repentance*. If God merely warned sinful people of impending judgment and then immediately carried it out, the warning would be no more than a cruel charade. On the contrary, our patient and loving God is generous in giving us plenty of time to repent. Though the Holy Spirit "will not contend with man forever" (Gen. 6:3), He will nevertheless contend and plead with him for a considerable period of time. In the case of the Flood it was "a hundred and twenty years" (6:3), an ample length of time indeed when we think of the depths of sin that depraved human ingenuity had plumbed during those days.

Fourth, *God always follows through on His decision to judge unless man repents*. Apart from man's sincere remorse for his sinful deeds and apart from his willingness to confess them, God always implements His warnings of judgment. He said that He would send rain on the earth for 40 days and 40 nights (see 7:4), and He did so (see 7:12). He said that He would wipe from the face of the earth every living creature He had made (see 7:4), and He did so (see 7:23). Our God can be counted on to fulfill every promise He makes, even when they are promises of judgment. When His people refuse to respond to His warnings, God's judgments are both inevitable and irreversible.

Fifth, *God's judgments always result in death*. His announcements of impending judgment are serious indeed and although death may not be the immediate result of His judgments it is always the ultimate result. In the case of the flood, there is scarcely room for doubt that both spiritual and physical death are intended. The animals and birds may have experienced only physical death, but wicked mankind surely experienced both. Just as eternal life is a gift from God, so also "the wages of sin is death" (Rom. 6:23)—eternal death.

Sixth, *God judges because He is just*. "Do not be deceived: God cannot be mocked. A man reaps what he sows" (Gal. 6:7). For God not to judge sin would be to make a mockery of justice. Since God is love, He grants salvation to the righteous; because He is just, He judges the sinner. The Flood stands forever as a vivid reminder of the latter principle.

In the words of Sir Thomas Browne: "That there was a Deluge once seems not to me to be so great a miracle as that there is not always one."

The Flood Ceases (Gen. 8:1-14)

"Water, water everywhere," cried the ancient mariner—and the ark floated on its surface (see Gen. 7:18). For five long months Noah and his family and all the animals rode out the flood (see 7:24). During that entire time they saw no dry land at all. They must have had the sinking feeling that God had forgotten them.

"But God remembered Noah" (8:1). Just when all seemed lost, God paid attention to Noah and lavished His loving care on him—for that is what the verb "remember" means in the Old Testament. To remember in the biblical sense of that term is not merely to recall to mind or to refresh one's memory. To remember someone means to express concern for him, to visit him with gracious love.

"God remembered Rachel," and she gave birth to a son whom she named Joseph (Gen. 30:22). Though even a mother may forget the baby at her breast, the Lord never forgets His children (see Isa. 49:14,15). At Calvary the dying criminal asked Jesus to remember him, and Jesus assured him that He would (see Luke 23:42,43). When God remembers His people, He remembers them "with favor" (Neh. 5:19; 13:31).

The hinge of the flood story, the fulcrum on which the story is balanced, is Genesis 8:1. Up to this point things were getting progressively worse, but from this point on things gradually get better. And the reason they improve is because "God remembered Noah."

In a very real sense, the period after the Flood marks a new beginning for the human race. It is again the first day of the first month of the first year of a man's new life (see 8:13). And in a remarkable way the events of Genesis 8 parallel the events of Genesis 1 in their literary order:

> 8:1: God "sent a wind" over the earth (see 1:2; in Hebrew the word for *wind* is the same as the word for *Spirit*).
>
> 8:2: "The springs of the deep and the flood-gates of the heavens had been closed" (see 1:7: God "separated the water under the expanse from the water above it").
>
> 8:5: "The waters continued to recede . . . and . . . the tops of the mountains became visible" (see 1:9: "Let the water under the sky be gathered . . . , and let dry ground appear").
>
> 8:6: Noah "sent out a raven, and it kept flying back and forth" (see 1:20: "Let birds fly above the earth").
>
> 8:17: "Bring out every kind of living creature that is with you—the birds, the animals, and all the creatures that move along the ground" (see 1:25: "God made the wild animals . . . , the livestock . . . , and all the creatures that move along the ground").

Genesis 9 continues the series by giving us three more parallels:

> 9:1: "God blessed Noah and his sons, saying to them, 'Be fruitful and increase in number and

fill the earth' " (1:28 says almost exactly the same thing).

9:2: "The fear and dread of you will fall upon all the beasts of the earth and all the birds of the air, upon every creature that moves along the ground, and upon all the fish of the sea" (see 1:28: "Rule over the fish of the sea and the birds of the air and over every living creature that moves on the ground").

9:3: "Just as I gave you the green plants, I now give you everything" (see 1:30: "I give every green plant for food").

Although other instructive and helpful comparisons could be made between Genesis 1 and Genesis 8, the events in question are not set forth in the same literary order in the two accounts. But the above examples illustrate the fact that Genesis 8 and 9 were deliberately structured with Genesis 1 in mind. The story of what took place as the floodwaters began to recede is the account of a *new creation* that parallels the account of the original creation in Genesis 1.

God remembered not only Noah and his family but also all the animals "that were with him in the ark" (8:1). Thousands of years later an angel of God said to Paul, who was in a sailing vessel on the storm-tossed Mediterranean, "God has graciously given you the lives of all who sail with you" (Acts 27:24). As the salt of the earth and the light of the world, God's people can sanctify those around them as well as influence them for good.

The Lord sent a wind to make the waters recede (see Gen. 8:1), but He can accomplish the same result simply by speaking a word of command (see Isa. 44:27; Nah. 1:4). During a furious storm on the Sea of Galilee, Jesus rebuked the winds and the waves and all became calm. Failing to recognize His deity, His disciples exclaimed, "What kind of man is this? Even the winds and the waves obey him" (Matt. 8:24-27). For God the Father and God the Son, easy mastery over wind and wave is routine (see Matt. 14:22-33).

Noah's ark eventually "came to rest on the mountains of Ararat" (Gen. 8:4). The kingdom of Ararat (called Urartu by the Assyrians in later times) is mentioned in Isaiah 37:38; 2 Kings 19:37; and Jeremiah 51:27. Urartu was an extensive and mountainous kingdom including much of the region north of Mesopotamia and east of modern Turkey, and encompassing the headwaters of the Euphrates as well as Lake Van and Lake Urmia. The landing site of Noah's ark was probably in southern Urartu rather than in northern Urartu. In any event, the peak known today as Mount Ararat, in northeastern Turkey on the Soviet border, has no better claim than any other mountain to be the place where the ark settled, since Genesis 8:4 states only that it came to rest somewhere on the "mountains" (plural) of Ararat (see chapter 11).

Four times Noah sent out birds from the ark to find out whether there was dry land in the vicinity. The third and fourth times produced positive results: First the dove returned carrying a "freshly plucked olive leaf" in its beak (8:11), proving to Noah that the waters had receded from the earth sufficiently enough to enable plants to grow again; and when the dove went out seven days later it did not return to Noah because it had found its own nesting place (see 8:12), perhaps at the mouth of a cave for protection and shelter (see Jer. 48:28).

Small wonder, indeed, that the dove should sometimes serve as a symbol of the Holy Spirit in the New

Testament (see Matt. 3:16), or that a dove carrying an olive branch should be a modern symbol of peace!

After removing the covering of the ark to get a clearer idea of just how dry the ground actually was, Noah still had to wait for almost two more months before the earth would become completely dry, making it possible for him and his family and the animals to leave the ark in comfort and safety (see Gen. 8:13,14).

Leaving the Ark (Gen. 8:15-19)

God broke His yearlong silence by commanding Noah and his family to come out of the ark. All other human life had perished in the flood and Noah's descendants would form the seed plot for the new human race.

Though the rest of mankind had been judged, Noah and his family had been redeemed. God had brought His faithful children through the fearful trial of the flood by telling them specifically how to escape it and survive. Throughout the long ages of history the Lord has always rescued those who trust in Him because "God did not appoint us to suffer wrath but to receive salvation through our Lord Jesus Christ" (1 Thess. 5:9).

The animals shared Noah's deliverance and as they had entered the ark with him, so also they left the ark with him. They too had been saved from the flood and now they could once again fulfill the command to multiply and be fruitful and increase in number.

God would soon bless Noah and his sons with a similar command. But before that blessing was spoken the aged patriarch would worship the Lord by building an altar to Him and sacrificing offerings on it. Worship and fellowship would blend in joyful celebration as a redeemed man and a redeeming God communed together.

11

THE FLOOD: UNIVERSAL OR LOCAL?

One of the most intriguing and difficult questions that every serious student of the Bible must try to answer for himself sooner or later is this: How extensive was Noah's flood? Did the floodwaters cover the entire globe or was only a portion of the ancient Near East under water?

Some readers of the book of Genesis, of course, would consider the above distinction irrelevant. They believe that the biblical flood story is to be understood as a parable and, therefore, that the flood never really took place at all. The story has merely theological meaning, they say; it teaches us that God takes sin seriously and judges all who disobey Him.

Others claim that the biblical flood narrative is a myth or legend, a kind of fairy tale, related to other similar myths both ancient and modern. Such stories represent a mentality that is unsophisticated or primitive or childlike, we are told; their authors believed that a worldwide flood did in fact take place, but they were mistaken; at best, a local flood grew in the telling and was eventually exaggerated to a magnitude out of all proportion to its original size. But in any event, say the proponents of this view, whether the flood actually happened is not important; what really matters is what the story tells us about God (or the gods) and His (or their) relationship to ancient mankind.

Needless to say, we who believe that the great Flood occurred in space and time—that it was a genuine historical event of profound importance—must categorically reject the parabolic and mythical views. There are no indications in the text of Genesis that the flood story is either a myth or a parable. Furthermore, Noah is connected to the historical Adam by the Genesis 5 genealogy and to the historical Abraham by the Genesis 11 genealogy (see also Luke 3:34-38).

Our task in this chapter, then, will be to set forth the main arguments pro and con with respect to the two dominant views held by evangelical believers today: (1) Noah's flood was geographically worldwide; (2) Noah's flood was geographically restricted to a portion of the ancient Near East.

The Universal Flood Theory

Ten rather formidable arguments can be marshaled in favor of the idea that the great flood covered the whole earth. We will examine each of these in turn, first defending them and then challenging their validity.

Argument number one: *The depth of the waters as described in Genesis demands that the flood be worldwide.* "All the high mountains under the entire heavens were covered. The waters rose and covered the mountains to a depth of more than twenty feet" (7:19,20). The ark was "45 feet high" (6:15), so "more than twenty feet" probably refers to the draft of the ark. The world's highest mountains were covered by enough water to keep the ark from scraping bottom and grounding, no matter where it drifted.

But arguing that the admittedly universal language of the flood story demonstrates conclusively that the flood itself was universal in extent may turn out to be self-defeating. In the first place, universal language is often a literary device that is best interpreted phenomenally or optically—that is, from the limited standpoint of the eyewitness who writes the account. The biblical flood narrative, with its carefully recorded chronological notations and other details, reads like a logbook kept by Noah himself.[1] If so, the "high mountains" were mountains that he knew of or had heard of or could see, the low-lying eminences of Shinar or Babylon (see 11:2) rather than the lofty peaks of the Zagros or Caucasus ranges, or—even less likely—the Himalayas. Height, after all, is a relative matter. If Noah was accustomed to living in the plains, "high mountains" for him were not necessarily alps. And we may justifiably apply the same principle to the other universal terms in the narrative: The "entire heavens" would mean all the heavens that Noah knew (the sky within his immediate perception or vision); "all" would mean only everything that he could perceive; the *earth* would mean only the earth that Noah experienced, better translated as *land* (the Hebrew word for *earth* in the Genesis flood story means *land*—a much more limited term than earth—in 80 percent of its occurrences in the Old Testament, and there is no reason that it could not mean *land* throughout the flood story as well); and so forth.

Second, universal language is often the language of hyperbole, the language of deliberate exaggeration for literary effect. Joel 3:2 refers to "all nations," but the context limits the phrase to the nations surrounding Jerusalem and Judah (see also Gen. 41:57; 2 Chron. 36:23; Dan. 2:37,38). Note especially Colossians 1:23, which states that the gospel "has been proclaimed to every creature under heaven."

An excellent modern example of hyperbolic language used to describe a flood by those who experienced it is the devastating deluge that struck Tunisia in 1969. The actual facts are these: The flood ravaged 80 percent of the land, more than 250,000 Tunisians fled their homes, 100,000 temporarily lost their homes to the floodwaters, at least 542 died, and 14 percent of the country's cattle and sheep were drowned. The flood was caused by torrential rains that poured down for two months with scarcely a break. And how did the flood victims themselves describe the disaster? It was "the flood of a thousand years," said one. "It was like the end of the world," said another.[2] If such language can be used to vividly portray the Tunisian flood of 1969, how much more is such language appropriate to describe the vastly greater flood of Noah's day!

Third, the chronology of the biblical flood story will not support a depth of more than a few hundred feet of water. One scholar has estimated (generously, we believe) that it took 324 days for the floodwaters to run off and completely dry up. At the reasonable runoff rate of four inches a day, the flood would have been only 108 feet deep—terribly destructive, to be sure, even at that. If we double the rate of runoff, the flood would have been 216 feet deep—still more destructive. But now let us assume for the sake of the argument that the *present* Mount Ararat (more on this later) was the site of the ark's landfall. Ararat's 17,000 feet divided by 324 days yields a daily average runoff rate of 52½ *feet*—caused only by a "wind" sent by God (8:1)! Water moving at that speed would doubtless have so severely damaged the earth's surface that it would have been virtually impossible to cultivate it for quite some time. And if we insist on understanding the universal language of the account literally, we would observe that the highest mountain known is Everest, forcing us to double the 17,000-foot figure and making the runoff problem twice as difficult.

Fourth, it has been calculated that if the Genesis flood story uses literal language throughout, to cover the highest mountains would require eight times more water than the world now contains. Question: Where did all those floodwaters run off to? An attempt to drain off so much water, especially in such a relatively short period of time, would prove to be impossible, it would seem.

Other questions immediately suggest themselves: If our entire planet was at one time covered with a sheath of water several miles thick, would astronomers not be able to detect its effects on astral history caused by the temporary increase of the earth's mass? Would not that much water have left visible marks on the earth's surface as well? Would not the indiscriminate mingling of fresh water and salt water all over the world have caused irreparable damage to nearly all forms of marine and freshwater life?

Argument number two: *Water always seeks its own level, and since the highest mountains in the Near East were covered, the highest mountains in the rest of the world were covered also*. The highest mountains in the Near East are well over 10 thousand feet tall, and therefore the flood must have been worldwide.

The validity of this argument, however, is closely tied to that of the previous one. We would of course agree that water always seeks its own level. But it may well be that the area covered by Noah's flood included mountains rising to only a few hundred feet, as the most plausible runoff rate of the floodwaters would seem to indicate. One or more of the extensive natural basins in the ancient Tigris-Euphrates flood plain would have been a suitable locale.[3] The region would most likely have included at least the southeastern part of Urartu (Ararat), where the mountains in ancient times may have been considerably lower than they are even today. In summary, until we can pinpoint the place where the ark landed (and we may never be able to do so) we will not be able to draw any conclusions about the universality of the flood based on the truism that water always seeks its own level.

Argument number three: *The flood lasted for over a year and was therefore universal.* While such a length of time is entirely in keeping with a worldwide flood, a local flood would have lasted for a few weeks at most.

One could argue just as strongly, however, that a universal flood—especially a flood during which the waters rose to a height of tens of thousands of feet—would require far longer than a year. The two months of rain during the 1969 Tunisian flood turned normally placid rivers into raging cataracts that crushed everything in their path. In the days of Noah, "the waters flooded the earth for a hundred and fifty days" (7:24). If the floodwaters covered the whole earth they rose at least a hundred feet a day during those five months. Such swiftly rising waters would have generated powerful currents that would have smashed the ark to smithereens against a cliff wall or mountainside. It will do no good to observe that "God remembered Noah" (8:1) and thus preserved the ark from such a calamity, because the sentence of which that phrase is a part is connected with the receding of the waters rather than with their rising. Obviously, then, a yearlong period of time is more suitable to a local flood—admittedly widespread and extensive—than to a universal flood. In the type of localized area described earlier, the floodwaters would have risen a couple of feet a day at the most during the five-month period and would not have threatened a huge ark in the least.

Argument number four: *The geology of the flood implies its universal extent*. The "springs of the great deep" (7:11) burst forth and continued to flood the continents of the world for five months, at the end of which they were closed (see 8:2). Such massive geologic upheavals imply a worldwide deluge and cannot be easily harmonized with the idea of a more localized flood.

But the fact is that we simply do not know how long the geological phenomena described in Genesis 7:11 lasted. It is entirely possible—indeed, contextually quite probable—that the verbs in 8:2 should be understood not in the past tense but in the pluperfect: "The springs of the deep and the floodgates of the heavens had been closed, and the rain had stopped falling from the sky." If that is so, the time span for the rising of the waters is reduced (perhaps considerably) making the theory of a local flood once again more attractive than that of a universal flood since reducing the time span increases the speed at which the waters must rise.

Proponents of a universal flood generally claim that all observable stratigraphic phenomena find a satisfactory explanation in the tremendous pressures built up during such a deluge. Some assert that even the world's oil deposits came into being during Noah's flood.[4] But most Christian geologists insist that although there is evidence for extensive local flooding in ancient times, no geological evidence whatever exists to prove the universal flood theory. And if a worldwide flood is the best way to account for the origin of oil, how was Noah able to coat the ark "with pitch inside and out" (6:14) before the Flood? The pitch Noah used was most likely "a natural derivative of crude petroleum."[5]

Argument number five: *The size of the ark compels us to assume that the flood was universal.* The ark's dimensions (see 6:15) are better calculated to serve the needs of tens of thousands of animals from all over the world than those of "only eight people and a few animals from the Near East."[6]

It would appear that the ark was indeed an enormous vessel (see chapter 9), although we would readily admit that we have no way of knowing for certain just how long Noah's cubit (his basic unit of measurement) actually was. If it was considerably shorter than the cubit of later times, the ark itself was much smaller than we have traditionally thought. But such speculation is fruitless except insofar as a smaller vessel and its animal cargo would have been much more easily serviced by eight people than a larger one would have.

A much more serious problem, however, for the universal flood theory arises in connection with the animal cargo itself. How would tens of thousands of species from all over the world get to the ark from their distant habitats? How would large land animals from other continents cross the oceans? Once in the ark, how could a mere eight people feed them and care for them? How could those people—or a much larger group of people, for that matter—provide the special diets and varied environments necessary?

Although very few animals hibernate, it has been suggested that practically all of the animals on the ark did so during the yearlong flood, freeing Noah and his family to perform other tasks. But if that is so, what are we to make of Genesis 6:21: "You are to take every kind of food that is to be eaten and store it away as food for you and for them"? It would seem to be clear that the animals in the ark were to masticate rather than hibernate during their yearlong voyage. And it would also seem to be much more likely that, no matter what the size of the ark, eight people cared for a smaller number of animals during a local flood than that eight people cared for thousands upon thousands of animals during a worldwide flood.

Argument number six: *No ark of any size would have been necessary unless the flood was universal.* If the impending flood was local, Noah and his family (and whatever animals would have been threatened with extinction) would have had plenty of time to move to a safe place out of reach of the floodwaters. They would also have been spared the enormous amount of labor involved in building the ark.

The ark, however, was more than simply a ship in which to ride out a flood. It was just as much a part of Noah's witness to his friends and neighbors as were his actual words. It served as a graphic warning to them that they could choose either to heed or to ignore.[7] A migration by Noah and his family would not have had nearly the same powerful effect. In fact other people might have joined them out of curiosity and escaped the flood in the bargain. The ark proved to be the best way to make absolutely certain that only Noah and his family would survive.

Argument number seven: *Second Peter 3:5-7 assumes that Noah's flood was universal.* Since creation (the subject of verse 5) was universal, and since the coming judgment (the subject of verse 7) will be universal, the flood (the subject of verse 6) was also universal. If that were not so the comparison would break down.

But we would observe that while verses 5 and 7 speak of the heavens and the earth in a clearly universal sense, verse 6 tells us only that "the world of that time was deluged and destroyed." It almost seems as though Peter deliberately chose a different word (*kosmos*, here translated "world") in verse 6 to differentiate it from the earth (and heavens) of verses 5 and 7. If then on other grounds Noah's flood is understood as being local, the "world" of 2 Peter 3:6 would mean the world of mankind or the like in its broader biblical context.[8] And this leads us immediately to the next argument often used in support of a universal flood.

Argument number eight: *Since all mankind was destroyed, the flood must have been worldwide.* A local flood would have destroyed only a part of mankind, and the text of Genesis is insistent in its claim that all sinful people were destroyed and that only Noah and seven others survived.

Two possible responses come to mind in this connection: "All sinful people" or its equivalent could be understood, from Noah's perspective, to refer to all the people who lived in the section of the ancient Near East with which he was familiar. Or, if we date the flood early enough (see the subhead "The Local Flood Theory"), "all sinful people" or its equivalent could in fact mean all the people on earth, since it is generally conceded that the most ancient civilizations emerged in the Near East.

In either case the purpose of the flood was to destroy all sinful mankind from the standpoint of the writer's intention. It cannot be proved that the writer had in mind anyone other than the inhabitants of the ancient Near East. And Noah's flood did not need to be worldwide in order to destroy them.

Argument number nine: *Flood stories are found in cultures all over the world and that proves that the flood was universal.* There are about 150 such stories and they come from nearly every part of the world. If Noah's flood was local, why should flood stories of all sorts be so widespread?

We note immediately that not all of the flood stories have the same value or importance. Some of them are merely local adaptations of the Genesis flood story, the latter having been taught to this or that group of people by Christian missionaries. Others bear little or no resemblance to the Genesis flood account. But a substantial number still seem to be related to a greater or lesser degree to the story of Noah's flood as found in Genesis.

An important point, however, is rarely noticed in connection with all of these stories. In each case it is a *local* group of people, not a *faraway* group, who have survived the flood. If all (or even a few) of the stories are true, that would mean that local survivors all over the world started the local traditions, and that in turn would mean that the biblical story, which speaks of only one surviving family, is mistaken.[9] But since we always start with the presupposition that the biblical account is true, then the other stories are either fictional or based on local floods in the areas of their origin or corruptions of the biblical story. If they are the latter their ultimate origin is the Near East and, whether Noah's flood was local or universal, they were eventually brought to their present locations by survivors of that flood. Their widespread distribution therefore says nothing about whether the flood was universal or local.

Argument number ten: *Noah's ark can still be seen on Mount Ararat and since Ararat is 17,000 feet high the flood was universal.* Ancient reports from such diverse authors as Berossus and Josephus combine with modern reports of ark sightings to authenticate the continued existence of Noah's ark. Fragments of wood from the ark brought down from Ararat by Fernand Navarra, an intrepid explorer, were shown to be 5,000 years old when first subjected to scientific analysis.[10]

As we have seen, however, the designation of Mount Ararat as the landing site for Noah's ark is highly suspicious. In the flood story itself we are told only that "the ark came to rest on the mountains of Ararat" (Gen. 8:4)—that is, ancient Urartu, an extensive region (see chapter 10). Furthermore, there is good reason to believe that the mountain today called Ararat did not receive that name until just a few hundred years ago.[11] Recent radiocarbon tests performed on Navarra's fragments indicate that they are only 1,200 to 1,500 years old, which means that the structure on Ararat claimed to be Noah's ark is probably a replica built by Byzantine monks.[12] An American expedition of 11 men hoping to get a closer look in July of 1970 was turned back by the Turkish government because the mountain is so close to Turkey's border with Russia. Since that time Turkey has routinely denied all requests to make the climb.

In any event, the "freshly plucked olive leaf" brought

to Noah by the dove (8:11) virtually rules out Ararat as the ark's landfall since olive trees do not grow within thousands of feet of that high elevation. In fact that one olive leaf may turn out to be the Achilles' heel of the universal flood theory because it implies that somewhere an olive tree had survived the flood (probably atop a relatively low mountain).

The Local Flood Theory

We have tried to show that the 10 major arguments for the universal flood theory, far from proving that the flood was universal, actually tend to support the local flood theory. While most Christian geologists affirm that the earth's strata bear no traces of a universal flood, archaeologists and other scientists have unearthed abundant evidence that there were many widespread and extensive local floods in antiquity. In fact we have an embarrassment of riches in this regard. Various reports, to give just a few examples, would date the flood (Noah's, or one similar to it) at about 10,000 B.C.[13] or 8500 B.C.[14] or 6500 B.C.,[15] each time caused primarily by the melting of polar ice caps.

A much more likely candidate for the biblical deluge, however, is the devastating flood that swept through the city of Ur in about 3500 B.C. It left an eight-foot-thick deposit of clean uniform clay in its wake.[16] Later floods that inundated the same general area appear not to have been quite so destructive, at least so far as the archaeological evidence goes. When we remember that Ur was Abraham's hometown (see 11:28,31; 15:7), the identification becomes even more attractive. Abraham may have brought the flood account with him to Canaan, where it became a part of the inspired biblical tradition as mediated to God's people through Moses.

Although in our judgment the evidence in Genesis favors the local flood theory over the universal flood theory, and although in our judgment other evidence tends to do the same, we do not wish to be dogmatic about our findings. Nor do we wish to reduce in any way the strong element of miracle that permeates the biblical account. But we believe that the sovereign God of the universe used the principle of the economy of miracle by choosing to employ a devastating, widespread and extensive but geographically restricted flood in destroying sinful mankind.

And when all is said and done, we find ourselves in agreement with the following assessment:

> The predominance of qualified Christian scholarship appears to favor a local flood interpretation because of the lack of evidence for and the problems attendant on a universal flood. . . . In the final analysis the true interpretation of the Biblical flood account will fully accord with true science. At this time we may favor one viewpoint over another but must seek continually to integrate all the pertinent data which seem well established.[17]

Notes

1. A.C. Custance, *The Flood: Local or Global?* (Grand Rapids: Zondervan Publishing House, 1979), p. 25.
2. *Newsweek* magazine (December 22, 1969), p. 34.
3. For a similar suggestion see B. Ramm, *The Christian View of Science and Scripture* (Grand Rapids: Wm. B. Eerdmans Publishing Company, 1954), p. 239.
4. H.M. Morris and J.C. Whitcomb, Jr., *The Genesis Flood* (Phil-

adelphia: The Presbyterian and Reformed Publishing Company, 1961), p. 434.

5. T.C. Mitchell in *The New Bible Dictionary*, J.D. Douglas, ed. (Grand Rapids: Wm. B. Eerdmans Publishing Company, 1962), p. 159.

6. J.C. Whitcomb, Jr., in *His* magazine (May, 1958), p. 38.

7. A.C. Custance, *op. cit.*, pp. 33-35.

8. W.F. Arndt and F.W. Gingrich, *A Greek-English Lexicon of the New Testament* (Chicago: The University of Chicago Press, 1957), p. 447.

9. A.C. Custance, *op. cit.*, p. 33.

10. E. Yamauchi in *Eternity* magazine (February, 1978), p. 29.

11. W. F. Albright as quoted in *St. Paul Pioneer Press* (February 22, 1970), sec. 3, p. 17.

12. *Newsweek* magazine (January 31, 1977), p. 56.

13. W. F. Albright, *Yahweh and the Gods of Canaan* (Garden City, New York: Doubleday & Company, Inc., 1968), p. 99.

14. *Christianity Today* magazine (November 7, 1975), p. 14.

15. *Christianity Today* magazine (September 10, 1976), p. 74.

16. J. Finegan, *Light from the Ancient Past* (Princeton: Princeton University Press, 1959), 2nd ed., pp. 27,28.

17. W.U. Ault in *The Zondervan Pictorial Encyclopedia of the Bible*, M.C. Tenney, ed. (Grand Rapids: Zondervan Publishing Company, 1975), vol. 2, p. 563.

12

THE FLOOD'S AFTERMATH

Genesis 8:20—9:29

As we noted in chapter 10, the receding of the floodwaters gave mankind the opportunity for a brand-new start. Even one of the dates in Noah's logbook signaled the beginning of a new era: "By the first day of the first month of Noah's six hundred and first year, the water had dried up from the earth" (Gen. 8:13). More than any other event since Creation itself, the aftermath of the great Flood inaugurated a time of beginning again.

A New Promise (Gen. 8:20-22)

The first recorded acts of righteous Noah after he left the ark were building an altar and offering sacrifices on it. Abel, one of Noah's spiritual ancestors, had also offered an animal sacrifice to the Lord many centuries earlier (see 4:4). As in the case of Noah, Abel's offerings pleased the Lord; like Noah, Abel was a "righeous man" (Heb. 11:4). We are reminded again that the motivation of the worshiper is always more important than the method he uses in his worship. Jesus, for example, condemns the prayers of hypocrites (see Matt. 6:5), but "the prayer of a righteous man is powerful and effective" (Jas. 5:16).

Worship properly offered is a very personal matter. For that reason, it is to God as "the LORD" that Noah brings his sacrifice, and it is "the LORD" who responds to Noah's act of worship (Gen. 8:20,21). LORD is the intimate, redemptive name of God in the Old Testament (see chapter 3), and as such it is regularly used in contexts of worship and sacrifice (see again 4:4).

In a vivid word picture that is painted often in the Bible (see for example Exod. 29:18,25), the Lord is portrayed as smelling the "pleasing aroma" of Noah's offering (Gen. 8:21). This is a beautiful way of expressing the delight that God takes in His children when they worship Him "in spirit and truth" (John 4:23). The image of an aroma has many practical applications, as when Paul says that "Christ loved us and gave himself up for us as a fragrant offering and sacrifice to God" (Eph. 5:2) or that gifts sent to him by the Christians at Philippi "are a fragrant offering, an acceptable sacrifice, pleasing to God" (Phil. 4:18). It can be a double-edged image as well, of course, because believers who are "the aroma of Christ" are at one and the same time "the fragrance of life" to those who are being saved and "the smell of death" to those who are perishing (2 Cor. 2:15,16).

The new promise solemnized by Noah's offering and symbolized by the Lord's response is that God will never again curse the ground or destroy all living creatures because of man (see Gen. 8:21). He had sent the great Flood because of the evil inclinations of the thoughts of men's hearts (see 6:5) but He will never do so again, "even though every inclination of [man's] heart is evil from childhood" (8:21). In an unforgettable way God had taught His people the lesson that sin inevitably brings judgment. No useful purpose would have been served by a divine decision to destroy mankind every few generations.

Therefore God promised that the normal cycles and processes of nature would continue unhindered "as long as the earth endures" (8:22). The functions of time and season mandated by God from the very beginning (see 1:14) would never again be interrupted until the end of history. The Lord's "covenant with day and night and the fixed laws of heaven and earth" (Jer. 33:25) would never cease. Like God's other universal promises, this one as well is to us and to our children.

New Commands (Gen. 9:1-7)

The divine judgment represented by the flood had issued in death for all mankind—all but the eight people in the ark. After the flood, however, "God blessed Noah and his sons" (9:1) by giving them three commands, either direct or implied, and all three have to do with life.[1]

First, *life will be propagated* (Gen. 9:1,7). The command to fill the earth that was given to man at the time of creation (see 1:28) is now repeated twice word for word: "Be fruitful and increase in number." It begins and ends the series of commands as if to emphasize the importance of multiplying the members of the human race in the shortest possible time.

Although the main purpose of the divine command was doubtless to populate the earth and give mankind the power to rule over it (see 9:2), large families in ancient times were not only a sign of God's favor but were also an economic necessity. In a largely agrarian culture, as many children as possible were needed to perform daily chores at an early age. The same situation obtains today in much of the Middle East.

The words of the psalmist, then, reflect practical reality as well as spiritual blessing: "Sons are a heritage from the LORD, children a reward from him. Like arrows in the hands of a warrior are sons born in one's youth. Blessed is the man whose quiver is full of them" (Ps. 127:3-5).

Second, *life will be sustained* (Gen. 9:2-4). Man would rule over the entire animal kingdom, which would be given into his hands. One of the uses to which various animals would be put would be to serve as food for mankind. It would seem that until the time of the Flood both men and animals were vegetarians (see 1:29,30). Now, however, animal meat would supplement man's diet (see 9:3).

Later in Israel's history a distinction would be made between clean and unclean animals, the former alone being considered ritually acceptable for human consumption (see Lev. 11). But during this earlier period, Noah and his sons were given only one restriction: "You must not eat meat that has its lifeblood still in it" (Gen. 9:4). Since "the life of every creature is its blood" (Lev. 17:14 stresses this principle by stating it twice), the severest penalties are inflicted on all who eat meat that still has its blood in it (see 17:10,14).

But blood is supremely important for another reason as well: "It is the blood that makes atonement for one's life" (Lev. 17:11). Although "it is impossible for the blood of bulls and goats to take away sins" (Heb. 10:4) in the ultimate sense it is equally true that "without the shedding of blood there is no forgiveness" (Heb. 9:22). When Jesus died on the cross for us, He poured out His lifeblood so that we might have life. In God's perfect plan, Christ's blood poured out in death was the only possible price that could be paid for our salvation, because "it is the blood that makes atonement for one's life."

Third, *life will be protected* (Gen. 9:5,6). Man and beast alike would be held accountable for the lives of any human beings they killed. This principle would later be formalized in the Law of Moses (see Exod. 20:13; 21:12,28,29).

God's command in Genesis 9:6 gives man not only the right but also the responsibility to put murderers to death. The reason is clear: God has made man in His own image and therefore the murderer, in taking the life of a man, displays contempt for God as well. This principle has important implications for the function of the state in the area of capital punishment. Civil government as instituted by God involves the power of life and death. It is not the mindless blood revenge of a murdered man's relatives but the orderly processes of civil law that should be the deciding factor in capital cases (see Num. 35:6-30). In this respect government, though a necessary evil because of human disobedience, is God's gracious provision for the preservation of human life (see Rom. 13:1-5; 1 Tim. 2:1-3; 1 Pet. 2:13-17).

A New Relationship (Gen. 9:8-17)

Life and the promise of its continued preservation is the theme of Genesis 9:8-17 as well. The covenant that God had earlier said He would establish with Noah (see 6:18) is now described in detail. As is the case with every other covenant in the Bible, God's covenant after the Flood is "with" His creatures (6:18; 9:9,10,11), "between" Himself and His creatures (9:12,13,15,16,17). A

covenant is an agreement that stresses relationship, and
with and *between* are the prepositions of relationship in
the Noahic covenant, the first leading logically and inevitably to the second. God establishes His covenant "with"
His creatures and it is then defined as a covenant "between" Him and them—a covenant that He binds Himself
to honor.

He establishes it and it is His from the outset. He
initiates it and places no limitations on it; it is both
unilateral and unconditional. Its provisions can be summed up in a single sentence: "Never again will all life be
cut off by the waters of a flood" (9:11).

The "never again" (see also 9:15) means that the
covenant is in force in perpetuity, "for all generations to
come" (9:12). It is, in short, "everlasting" (9:16). God,
"who does not change like shifting shadows" (Jas. 1:17),
pledges Himself never again to destroy all life by means
of a flood. Though we may be faithless, He remains
faithful (see 2 Tim. 2:13).

As a visible sign and seal of the provisions of His
covenant with Noah, God invested the rainbow with new
significance. From that time on, whenever it appeared in
the clouds it would serve as a reminder of God's covenant
with all His creatures (see Gen. 9:12-17). Just as circumcision would later become the sign of the Abrahamic
covenant (see 17:11) and just as the Sabbath would become the sign of the Sinaitic covenant (see Exod.
31:16,17), so also the rainbow is the sign of the Noahic
covenant for all time. And just as circumcision and the
Sabbath were in existence long before the institution of
the covenants they came to signify, so also the rainbow
almost certainly did not make its first appearance in the
days of Noah. Scientists tell us that there is clear evidence

of rainfall long before the time of Noah's flood (no matter how early we date it). But the rainbow was invested with new meaning in Genesis 9 and the believer who understands this fact should never be able to look at rainbows in quite the same way again. For others it may simply be a beautiful natural phenomenon, but for us it is in addition a perpetual reminder of God's covenant promise to Noah and his family and all the animals: Floodwaters will never again destroy all life.

A New Temptation (Gen. 9:18-23)

After a brief transitional paragraph we read the sordid account of how even a righteous man like Noah could fall into sin. Like his father Lamech (see 5:29), Noah was a farmer, a "man of soil" (9:20). Whether he "proceeded to plant a vineyard" or "was the first to plant a vineyard" (either translation is possible) the result was the same: He drank some of its wine and "became drunk" (9:21).

No serious student of Scripture can fail to be impressed by the fact that this first mention of wine in the Bible immediately points out its potentially devastating effects. Christians may differ as to whether the Scriptures teach temperance in the sense of abstinence or of moderation, but all must ultimately agree with the warning voiced by Solomon: "Wine is a mocker and beer a brawler; whoever is led astray by them is not wise" (Prov. 20:1). Because drunkenness often causes people to lower their defenses they can readily succumb to the basest forms of immorality, including incest (see Gen. 19:30-35).

In Noah's case the situation seems innocent enough at first—he was simply lying "uncovered inside his tent" (9:21). But although before the fall of man nakedness was not a cause for shame (see 2:25), afterward it was looked at in quite a different way (see 3:7,10,11,21). Ham, Noah's youngest son (see 9:24) and therefore perhaps somewhat brash and immature, "saw his father's nakedness and told his two brothers outside" (9:22). We have no way of knowing what Ham said to his brothers but we are left with the impression that mocking of some sort was involved. Shem and Japheth, being older and more mature, were determined not to bring further disgrace on their father. So they covered his nakedness with a garment and did not look at him.

A Final Word (Gen. 9:24-29)

Noah eventually awoke from his drunken stupor and discovered what Ham had done. He then uttered a prophecy that was to have far-reaching consequences for centuries to come.

The prophecy centers around Canaan, who was Ham's son (see 9:18,22). Children are often punished for the sins of their fathers (see Exod. 20:5) and Canaan was no exception. His special curse was that he would be the lowest of slaves to his brothers, and that fact is stated no less than three times in three verses (see Gen. 9:25-27).

We observe immediately that Noah's prophecy cannot be used to justify the enslavement of blacks by whites (such an interpretation was quite common in the nineteenth century and it is still found here and there even today).[2] As far as we know, Noah's three sons were all Caucasian. But even though some have argued that Ham was the progenitor (ultimately) of the black race, Noah did not curse Ham but Canaan—and the Canaanites were definitely Caucasian. Historically, the Canaanites were conquered and subdued by various peoples, including the

Israelites under Joshua. This is doubtless the main intent of Noah's prophecy.

Genesis 9 ends with a reminder that Noah was an outstanding member of the Genesis 5 genealogy. Like his forebears in that chapter, he lived to a very advanced age. Like Enoch, he had "walked with God" (5:21,23; 6:9) earlier in his life. If Noah had not fallen into sin after the flood, perhaps God would have taken him away as He did Enoch (see 5:24). But in Noah's case that was not to be. Like his other ancestors in Genesis 5, Noah died (see 9:29).

Notes

1. G. Vos, *Biblical Theology* (Grand Rapids: Wm. B. Eerdmans Publishing Company, 1948), p. 64.
2. C.T. Francisco, "The Curse on Canaan," *Christianity Today* magazine (April 24, 1964), pp. 8-10.

13

THE SPREAD OF THE NATIONS

Genesis 10:1—11:26

As Genesis 10 begins, Noah is dead but his sons are very much alive. The story of their role in fulfilling the divine command to "be fruitful and increase in number" (9:1,7) concludes the primeval history of 1:1—11:26. It is divided into two main sections: "the account of Shem, Ham and Japheth, Noah's sons" (10:1—11:9), and "the account of Shem" (11:10-26). The first section includes the story of the tower of Babel, a flashback narrative that gives us the main reason for the spread of the nations described in Genesis 10. Since 11:1-9 (the Babel account) is chronologically prior to 10:1-32, we will discuss it first.

The Confusion of Tongues (Gen. 11:1-9)

The story of the tower of Babel displays one of the finest examples of inverted or hourglass structure to be found anywhere in literature.[1] Genesis 11:1,2 parallels 11:8,9; both are narrative passages and both emphasize the fact that at one time the whole world had only one language. Genesis 11:3,4 matches 11:6,7; both consist totally of direct discourse, both highlight the phrase "Come, let us," and when taken together as a single unit they begin and end with the phrase "each other." Genesis 11:1-4 deals totally with what men did, and 11:6-9 deals totally with what God did in response. Genesis 11:5 is the narrow aperture of the hourglass that joins the upper and lower compartments. To change the image, just as 8:1 is the hinge of the Flood story (see chapter 10), so 11:5 is the hinge of the Babel account: "But the LORD came down to see the city and the tower that the men were building." Before that verse there was only human activity and after it there was only divine activity. As always, God had the final word.

As might be expected, the survivors of the great Flood spoke only one language. Their descendants eventually moved to Shinar (an ancient name for Babylonia) and settled there (see 11:2). They decided to build a city and a tower in order to make a name for themselves as well as to demonstrate their sense of unity. If they had been living in Palestine they would have used stone and mortar as building materials, but since they were in Babylonia they used brick and tar (see 11:3). There was very little stone available for use in building in ancient Mesopotamia, as the brick structures routinely excavated by archaeologists in that part of the world so vividly illustrate.

The tower built on the site was doubtless of a particular type known technically as a *ziggurat*. Square at the base, its sloping, stepped sides culminated in a small shrine at the top. The builders of the ziggurats often painted such shrines with blue enamel in order to make them blend in with the celestial home of one or more of their gods. They believed that a deity would live temporarily in the shrine when he came down to meet with his people. The worshiper would climb the outside staircase of the ziggurat all the way to the top in the hope that his god would condescend to meet with him in the little chapel there.

The story of Jacob's dream in 28:12 refers to "a stairway resting on the earth, with its top reaching to heaven." Similarly, Genesis 11 speaks of "a tower that reaches to the heavens" (11:4). Other Mesopotamian temple towers had comparable names, indicating that they were intended as staircases from earth to heaven. The one at Asshur was called The House of the Mountain of the Universe, Borsippa's tower was called The House of the Seven Guides of Heaven and Earth, and Larsa's people knew theirs as The House of the Link Between Heaven and Earth. The tower at Babel was referred to by the Babylonians themselves as The House of the Foundation-Platform of Heaven and Earth.[2] Partial restoration of the city of Babylon and the reconstruction of the tower there were topics discussed recently by the Iraqi government and Japan's Kyoto University.[3]

The original tower of Babel was a monument not to the one true God but to egotistical mankind: "Let *us* build *ourselves* a city, . . . so that *we* may make a name for *ourselves*" (11:4, italics added). Hardly the "cathedral of antiquity," as one author describes it,[4] the tower represented a prideful human attempt to storm the bastions of heaven and force the gods to bend to the will of man. And so the Lord Himself came down and effectively halted the construction project by confusing the language of the builders, making it impossible for them to communicate with one another.

The Akkadian word transcribed as *Babel* in 11:9

means literally "gateway to a god"—an apt description of
a ziggurat intended to connect heaven and earth. (Jacob's
ziggurat was similarly called "the gate of heaven"; see
28:17.) But the word *Babel* sounds enough like the Hebrew word *bālal*, "confused," to provide an opportunity
for an appropriate pun by the writer. To this day, a babel
of voices means a confusion of cries or other vocal
sounds. Though originally built to bring God and man
into joyful communion with each other (a feat successfully accomplished in Jacob's dream; see 28:15,16), the
tower of Babel ended in confusion and scattering. Such is
the inevitable fate of all such man-made schemes.

At the Constitutional Convention of 1787, Benjamin
Franklin quoted the *King James Version* of Psalm 127:1:
"Except the LORD build the house, they labor in vain that
build it." He then continued, "I firmly believe this, and I
also believe that without his concurring aid we shall
succeed in this political building no better than the builders of Babel."[5]

Babel was reversed on the Day of Pentecost when the
coming of the Holy Spirit restored linguistic harmony.
Galileans were suddenly heard speaking in a dozen different languages, "declaring the wonders of God" (Acts
2:11). Bewilderment always gives way to understanding
when we genuinely submit ourselves to the perfect will of
a loving God.

The Diffusion of Nations (Gen. 10:1-32)

Genesis 10 is often called the Table of Nations, but it
could just as easily and correctly be called a map of the
ancient Near East. In form it is a modified genealogy and
it uses the words *son* and *father* even more flexibly than in
the genealogies of Genesis 4; 5; and 11. *Son* in Genesis 10

may mean descendant, successor or nation; and *father* may mean ancestor, predecessor or founder. In content Genesis 10 describes the end results of the scattering of mankind caused by the debacle at the tower of Babel (see 11:1-9).

The nations of the then-known world are divided into three broad categories corresponding to the three sons of Noah. The Japhethites are listed first, possibly because Japheth was the oldest of the three sons (see 10:21). The Shemites (later called Semites) are listed last because they were to be the progenitors of the chosen people. A separate genealogy is devoted to them in 11:10-26. The Hamites are listed second even though Ham was the youngest of Noah's three sons (see 9:24).

When we add up the nations that came from Shem, Ham and Japheth, we discover a very intriguing fact: The total number is 70 (14 from Japheth, 30 from Ham and 26 from Shem). This is a further example of the sevens and tens and seventies that we have observed so often up to this point in the text of Genesis. But it is more: It would also seem to be an anticipation of the number of the members of Jacob's family in Egypt, who were "seventy in all" (46:27; Exod. 1:5). The 70 nations of Genesis 10 are conveniently summarized in 1 Chronicles 1:5-23 where they are listed in exactly the same order.

By and large, the Japhethites lived far to the north and west of Palestine and spoke Indo-European languages. The people of Gomer and the associated nations of Ashkenaz, Riphath and Togarmah (see Gen. 10:3) lived around the Black Sea. The name Gomer is reflected in the later Cimmerians, while Ashkenaz became the Scythians of later times. Magog lived north of the Caspian Sea, and the southern shores of the Black Sea provided a home for

Tubal and Meshech (not related to modern Tobolsk and Moscow in the Soviet Union, as is sometimes claimed). These three nations are all mentioned in Assyrian inscriptions of a later period as well as in Ezekiel 38:2. Tiras is probably Thrace, located west of the Black Sea. Madai, the Medes, lived south of the Caspian Sea in the later history of the area. .

Associated with Javan (Ionia, the southern part of Greece) were "Elishah, Tarshish, the Kittim and the Rodanim" (Gen. 10:4). Elishah may refer to Sicily and southern Italy, or perhaps to Alashia, an ancient name for Crete. Tarshish is probably southern Spain, while the Kittim lived on the island of Cyprus. The word Rodanim is perhaps reflected in Rhodes, one of the Greek isles.

Genesis 10:5 (see also 10:20,31) indicates that the criteria for distinguishing the various groups from each other were rather complex. *Territories* is a geographic term, *clans* an ethnic term, *nations* a political term and *language* a linguistic term. This may explain why Canaan, for example, is listed under Ham (which exerted strong political influence over Canaan very often in ancient times—see 9:18,22,24-27) instead of under Shem (to whom Canaan is much more closely related linguistically). It may also explain why some nations are listed twice: Sheba appears under both Ham (see 10:7) and Shem (see 10:28), as does Havilah (see 10:7,29). It is also possible, of course, that there was more than one Sheba and more than one Havilah.

The Hamites migrated for the most part to northeast Africa, the eastern Mediterranean region, and southern Arabia. Cush in 10:6,7 is the territory of the upper Nile south of Egypt. Related nations in southern Arabia were Seba, Havilah, Sabtah, Raamah, Sabtecah, Sheba and

Dedan. Raamah, Sheba and Dedan (see 10:7) reappear in Ezekiel 27:20-22, while Sheba and Dedan (or their name-sakes) occur as the names of two of Abraham's grandsons in Genesis 25:3. Sabtah and Sabtecah are perhaps reflected in the names of two later Egyptian pharaohs.

A second Cush (see 10:8) was located in central and southern Mesopotamia. Its name may be related to that of the later Kassite kingdom. Nimrod is perhaps the Hebrew name of Sargon the Great of the city of Akkad. A mighty warrior and hunter, he is obviously intended as an individual historical figure in this passage. Among other cities under his rule were Babylon, Erech (called Uruk by the ancient Babylonians), Nineveh and Calah.

Mizraim is the Hebrew word for Egypt. It means literally *two Egypts* and referred historically to Upper Egypt and Lower Egypt. Middle Egypt was inhabited by the Pathrusites (see 10:14). Other nations frequently under the control of Egypt were the Ludites (possibly the Lydians in Asia Minor, although this is by no means certain), the Lehabites (possibly the inhabitants of the Lybian desert), the Casluhites (ancestors of certain Philistine groups), and the Caphtorites (Caphtor, another name for Crete, was the original homeland of other Philistine groups—see Jer. 47:4; Amos 9:7).

Canaan (later called *Palestine* after the Philistines) included a number of well-known tribes and nations. Among them were the people of Sidon, the port city on the northern coast. The Hittites eventually became one of the most powerful nations in the entire region, mainly because of their monopoly in the smelting of iron (see chapter 7). The Jebusites were the original inhabitants of Jerusalem, while the Amorites (the name comes from a Babylonian word meaning westerner) lived in other parts

of the hill country. Most of the lesser-known groups
(Gen. 10:16-18) lived in small city-states. Especially
interesting is the almost incidental mention of Sodom,
Gomorrah, Admah and Zeboiim (see 10:19), four of the
five cities of the plain referred to in 14:2,8. Sodom and
Gomorrah in particular are now known to have been very
ancient cities. Their names have been found in the Ebla
tablets, recently excavated in northern Syria and dating to
about 2400 B.C.

Although Eber occurs as a name far down the list
among the Shemites (Semites), his importance is called to
our attention early in the passage: "Shem was the ancestor
of all the sons of Eber" (10:21). Since *Eber* is related to
the word *Hebrew,* it is generally agreed that he was the
ancestor of the Hebrew people. Amazingly enough, his
name has also turned up in the Ebla tablets in the form
Ebrium, a king who ruled over Ebla for 28 years.[6] One can
only speculate, however, as to whether King Ebrium and
the biblical Eber are one and the same person.

Most of the nations associated with Shem are well
known indeed. The Elamites lived between the Medes to
the north and the Persian Gulf to the south. Asshur
(Assyria) was northern Mesopotamia, while Arphaxad
(perhaps Chaldea) was probably southern Mesopotamia.
Lud is almost surely the Lydians of Asia Minor, and the
Arameans lived in the land known today as Syria.

One of Eber's sons was named Peleg (a Hebrew word
meaning *division*), "because in his time the earth was
divided" (10:25). Various geological phenomena of a
catastrophic nature have been read into this verse, but the
language is so general that we cannot even be sure what
kind of division (physical? geographical? spiritual? so-
cial?) is intended.

Joktan lived in southern Arabia, and three of the 13 nations associated with him are of special interest. Hazarmaveth survives in the term *Hadhramautic,* one of the most important dialects of the South Arabic language. Sheba is famous as the homeland of the queen that visited Solomon in the tenth century B.C. (see 1 Kings 10:1-13). And Ophir was the source of much of the gold in which Solomon traded (see 9:28; 10:11).

Genesis 10 is a remarkable chapter indeed. Scholars continue to be fascinated by the wealth of geographic knowledge it contains, and Bible students of all ages long to visit its faraway places and thrill to its strange-sounding names. A true map of oriental lands, it is without peer for its time. And it reminds us that mankind, however fragmented and alienated, has a common origin in the ancient past.

The First Semitic Genealogy (Gen. 11:10-26)

"The account of Shem," however brief, is the fifth main section of the primeval history in Genesis (see chapter 1). Like the Genesis 5 genealogy, Genesis 11:10-26 consists of exactly 10 names. As the Genesis 5 genealogy begins and ends with a famous name (Adam, Noah), so the Genesis 11 genealogy does the same (Shem, Abram). And as the 10 names of the Genesis 5 genealogy are conveniently summarized in 1 Chronicles 1:1-3, so the 10 names in the Genesis 11 list are summarized in 1 Chronicles 1:24-27. Half of the names in the Genesis 11 genealogy appear in the same order in 10:21-25, where additional details are also given.

Two major differences between the genealogies in Genesis 5 and 11 are that the former (1) gives total figures for the ages of the men at death, and (2) concludes nearly every paragraph with the phrase "and then he died." The main purpose of the Genesis 11 genealogy seems to be to provide the briefest possible transition between Shem and Abram, and so the author omitted all but the most important facts.

The first Semitic genealogy ends by telling us that Terah "became the father of Abram, Nahor and Haran" (11:26), the latter dying while his father was still alive (see 11:28). In commenting on Abraham's pagan background, Joshua 24:2 states that Isarel's forefathers, "including Terah the father of Abraham and Nahor, . . . worshiped other gods." It was from such an idolatrous environment that God called Abraham (see Gen. 12:1)—a call that Abraham obeyed without hesitation (see 12:4).

But that story, a story of yet another new and exciting venture of faith, a story known as the patriarchal history, begins where the primeval history ends.[7]

Notes

1. I.M. Kikawada, "The Shape of Genesis 11:1-9," in *Rhetorical Criticism: Essays in Honor of James Muilenburg*, J.J. Jackson and M. Kessler, eds. (Pittsburgh: The Pickwick Press, 1974), pp. 18-32.
2. R. Youngblood, *Faith of Our Fathers* (Ventura, CA: G/L Publications, 1976), pp. 82,83.
3. *Christianity Today* magazine (February 22, 1980), p. 53.
4. A. Parrot, *The Tower of Babel* (New York: Philosophical Library, 1955), p. 68.
5. *Decision* magazine (June, 1976), p. 9.
6. *National Geographic* magazine (December, 1978), p. 755.
7. See R. Youngblood, *Faith of Our Fathers* (Ventura, CA: G/L Publications, 1976), a Bible commentary for laymen on Genesis 12—50 in the same series as the present volume.

BIBLIOGRAPHY

(Inclusion of a book in the following list does not necessarily indicate wholesale approval of the author's viewpoint or methodology.)

Albright, William F. *Yahweh and the Gods of Canaan*. Garden City, New York: Doubleday & Company, Inc., 1968.

Cassuto, U. *A Commentary on the Book of Genesis. Part I: From Adam to Noah*. Jerusalem: The Magnes Press, 1961. *Part II: From Noah to Abraham*. Jerusalem: The Magnes Press, 1964.

Davis, John J. *Paradise to Prison*. Grand Rapids: Baker Book House, 1975.

Douglas, J.D., ed. *The New Bible Dictionary*. Grand Rapids: Wm. B. Eerdmans Publishing Company, 1962.

Griffith Thomas, W.H. *Genesis: A Devotional Commentary*. Grand Rapids: Wm. B. Eerdmans Publishing Company, 1946.

Kidner, Derek. *Genesis*. Downers Grove, IL: Inter-Varsity Press, 1967.

Kitchen, K.A. *Ancient Orient and Old Testament*. Chicago: Inter-Varsity Press, 1966.

Parrot, André. *The Tower of Babel*. New York: Philosophical Library, 1955.

Pritchard, James B., ed. *Ancient Near Eastern Texts Relating to the Old Testament*, 2nd ed. Princeton, NJ: Princeton University Press, 1955.

Ramm, Bernard. *The Christian View of Science and Scripture*. Grand Rapids: Wm. B. Eerdmans Publishing Company, 1954.

Sarna, Nahum M. *Understanding Genesis*. New York: Schocken Books, 1966.

Schaeffer, Francis A. *Genesis in Space and Time*. Downers Grove, IL: Inter-Varsity Press, 1972.

Speiser, E.A. *Genesis*. Garden City, NY: Doubleday & Company, Inc., 1964.

Vos, Geerhardus. *Biblical Theology*. Grand Rapids: Wm. B. Eerdmans Publishing Company, 1948.

Whitcomb, John C. Jr., and Morris, Henry. *The Genesis Flood*. Philadelphia: The Presbyterian and Reformed Publishing Company, 1961.

Wiseman, P.J. *Clues to Creation in Genesis*. Donald J. Wiseman, editor. London, England: Marshall, Morgan & Scott, 1977.

Youngblood, Ronald. *Faith of Our Fathers*. Ventura, CA: G/L Publications, 1976.

———, *The Heart of the Old Testament*. Grand Rapids: Baker Book House, 1971.